Praise for *Power in Precision*

"In the dynamic marketplace of politics and advocacy, the ability to articulate ideas with clarity and conviction is paramount. *Power in Precision* serves as an indispensable guide for writers aiming to advance economic freedom and influence policy. This book provides practical ways to transform complex economic concepts into persuasive, accessible narratives that can shape public opinion and drive policy change."

— Eamonn Butler, Director and Cofounder, Adam Smith Institute

"Overall *Power in Precision* is very well done. Aligning what you think with what you say and what you write so that others understand you precisely and exactly is an art and a science that few learn and even fewer teach. This book guides the way."

— Nicholas Donofrio, IBM Fellow Emeritus, former IBM Executive Vice President, Innovation and Technology, and Author, *If Nothing Changes, Nothing Changes.*

"*Power in Precision* is the inaugural book in a series dedicated to mastering effective communication, making it a vital addition to any professional's collection. This guide will assist you in crafting clear, jargon-free messages that are both persuasive and engaging, perfectly tailored to your audience."

— Patrick Finnegan, Senior Health and Pharma Credit Analyst, Former Board Member, International Accounting Standards Board, and Former Partner, Deloitte & Touche.

"In the boom of today's creator economy, storytelling and editorial remain key to connecting with your community. *Power In Precision* will equip astute marketers, influencers, operators, and sales folks with the tools to deliver effective and impactful narrative. While images are wonderful, it is the combination of highly organized words that can make a difference in building brands and communities."

— Matthew I. Growney, Creative Director & Founder, Thermal Brands.

"The ability to convey complex financial information clearly, accurately and cogently is a critical skill. *Power in Precision* enables accounting and finance professionals who strive to move beyond the numbers to craft persuasive analyses and compelling stories that resonate with investors and other stakeholders."

— Robert Herz, Board Member and Former Chair, Financial Accounting Standards Board, Former Executive-in-Residence, Columbia Business School, and Former Partner, PricewaterhouseCoopers.

"Boards of directors require candid, concise communications of the significant issues that should be understood and considered. Unfortunately, most board materials are very lengthy, and important matters can unitentionally get lost in details. *Power in Precision* offers practical, straightforward advice for creating clear, succinct board materials that directors want and need. Finance professionals and auditors striving to more effectively communicate key issues and judgments to boards and committees would greatly benefit from this valuable guidance.

— Olivia F. Kirtley, Corporate Board Member, Former Chair, American Institute of Certified Public Accountants (AICPA), Former President, International Federation of Accountants (IFAC), and Former CFO.

"In international financial institutions, where decisions affect billions of people across the globe, being able to inform, build consensus and inspire diverse stakeholders into action is critical. *Power in Precision* guides leaders on using simple, structured, inclusive language to articulate today's complex, global problems in terms people understand, and to elicit support for strategies to address them."

— Bernard Lauwers, Finance Director, International Monetary Fund, and Former Senior Executive, The World Bank Group.

"Mark Watson's *Power in Precision* offers business economists and new writers a primer and a style guide on how to write more clearly and directly. We all need this as we draft memos for our CEOs, or prepare policymakers for testimony, or present to large general audiences. Watson's call for better writing is on target. Much we read today can be imprecise, turgid, and riddled with jargon or clichés. If you want to reach your audience by improving your writing skills, this book is for you."

— Stuart Mackintosh, International Economist, former Group of Thirty Executive Director, and Author, *Climate Crisis Economics* and *The Redesign of the Global Financial Architecture*.

"Mark Twain was attributed with the quote 'I wrote you a long letter as I did not have time to make it short.' It underscores the difficulty most of us have balancing being concise and insightful. *Power in Precision* helps the reader strike that balance to be able to deliver a clear and cogent message in an era of shortened attention spans. Highly recommend it for business and non-business communicators alike."

— Marty Pfinsgraff, Founder and CEO of MP Alpha Advisory, Board Director, and Former Financial Services Regulator and Executive.

Power in Precision

A Guide to Effective Business Writing

Power In Series

Effective communication is a reflection of your professional identity. If you want to set yourself apart as a leader and open doors to new opportunities, you need to hone your ability to communicate so you inform, persuade and inspire.

Already available

Power in Presence: A Guide to Effective Business Conversations

Power in Presence helps professionals develop the skills to project confidence, engage effectively in conversations and build meaningful connections, so they leave a lasting impact in both formal meetings and everyday discussions.

Forthcoming publications in the *Power In* Series

Power in Perception: A Guide to Effective Data Visualization

Power in Perception shows how to create clear and persuasive data visualizations that transform complex data into actionable insights, resulting in thoughtful decisions and better outcomes.

Power in Persuasion: A Guide to Effective Presentation

Power in Persuasion teaches professionals how to turn ideas into powerful, persuasive messages in the form of compelling presentations, stories and speeches that will resonate with myriad audiences.

You can access additional *Power In* series content by scanning the QR code or by visiting our website (www.powerinseries.com).

Power in Precision

A Guide to Effective Business Writing

Mark Watson

Inform. Persuade. Inspire.

Power in Precision: A Guide to Effective Business Writing

Self-Published by: Portcullis Consulting, LLC, Concord, MA

Copyright © 2024 by Mark Watson. All rights reserved.

Published in the United States of America.

First Edition

Editor: Francesca Forrest

Cover Design: Darcy Kelly-Laviolette

Inside Design: Kevin Sharkey

For more information about *Power in Precision*, visit www.powerinseries.com.

Publisher's Cataloging-in-Publication Data

Names: Watson, Mark, 1969-, author.

Title: Power in precision : a guide to effective business writing / Mark Watson.

Series: Power In Series

Description: Includes index. | First edition. | Concord, MA: Mark Watson, 2024.

Identifiers: ISBN: 979-8-9913615-2-1 (hardcover) | 979-8-9913615-1-4 (paperback) | 979-8-9913615-0-7 (ebook)

Subjects: LCSH Business writing. | Commercial correspondence. | BISAC BUSINESS & ECONOMICS / Business Writing | LANGUAGE ARTS & DISCIPLINES / Rhetoric | BUSINESS & ECONOMICS / Business Communication / General

Classification: LCC HF5718.3 .W38 2024 | DDC 808/.06665--dc23

Table of Contents

Introduction: Elevate Your Career Through Powerful Writing

Effective written communication is a cornerstone of success in today's business world. As you ascend the ranks, your ability to articulate ideas, strategies and visions becomes increasingly important. From the succinct clarity demanded in emails to the persuasive eloquence expected in proposals and presentations, the necessity of well-crafted writing permeates every aspect of your professional life. Even something so seemingly mundane as the bullet points in a PowerPoint presentation require care and attention.

Beyond the mere transmission of information, writing is an expression of your professional identity and brand. Neglecting to hone this skill can raise doubts among colleagues regarding your attention to detail and your competence in other areas. If, for example, you constantly confuse "e.g." and "i.e." or rely too heavily on complex prose, you risk damaging your credibility and may hinder your career progression, especially if colleagues keep resorting to redlining your drafts or taking over the writing process altogether.

Exceptional writing has the power to set you apart as a thought leader, elevate your standing among peers and open doors to new opportunities. Embracing the art of writing allows you to harness language to influence, persuade and inspire.

Despite the importance of writing, many professionals struggle to express their ideas clearly, especially as their knowledge deepens. The desire to convey every nuance or to qualify perspectives often results in dense, less compelling prose. Attempts to make writing stand out through the use of jargon, hyperbole or clichés often backfire: instead the writing becomes inaccessible, particularly in a global context.

Nowadays, we have the option of turning to artificial intelligence (AI) for help, but viewing AI as a panacea is a mistake. While AI undoubtedly accelerates the writing process, it often lacks the insight, depth and nuance characteristic of effective human communication. Without a foundation in effective writing, writers will struggle to enhance the output generated by AI.

The objective of *Power in Precision* is to equip you with practical strategies to enhance your writing. Unlike conventional guides that inundate readers with complex grammatical terms and arbitrary style rules, this book prioritizes actionable advice. Recognizing that few professionals are familiar with grammar's intricacies, the book provides clear guidance in layman's terms (though Appendix 1 includes some basic terms for the interested reader). Furthermore, it demystifies common writing rules, empowering you to bend them with precision and intent, and to proactively avoid arcane grammar debates with colleagues and superiors.

As you progress through the book, you may encounter advice seemingly tailored for spoken rather than written language. This includes guidance on sporting metaphors and vogue terminology. While verbal clarity is crucial for career advancement, these concepts are discussed within a writing guide because they often infiltrate written communication, resulting in imprecise, hard-to-understand prose.

While a key message of *Power in Precision* is conciseness, the book unabashedly embraces its length. Rich with practical, easy-to-understand guidance and examples of effective and ineffective writing, it bridges the gap between theory and reality.

The book is structured as follows:

- **Part 1: Foundations of Effective Writing:** This part lays the groundwork for successful business writing, focusing on overcoming writer's block, structuring thoughts effectively with proven frameworks like Barbara Minto's *Pyramid Principle* and establishing a clear, persuasive narrative. It combines theory with practical techniques for transitioning ideas from conceptualization to paper.

- **Part 2: Advanced Writing Techniques:** Delving deeper, this part covers certain particulars of achieving clarity and precision in writing, including the active and passive voices, maintaining consistent tense, strategic use of modal verbs and the importance of verb choice to strengthen statements. This section also covers other grammar and punctuation particulars, as well as choosing the right tone, writing respectfully and keeping your writing simple and succinct.

- **Part 3: Data Presentation:** This part focuses on the effective use of visuals and data to complement and enhance written content. It provides strategies for data storytelling, the creative presentation of information and the use of structural techniques (e.g., subheadings and lists) to improve document readability and effect.

- **Part 4: Special Topics in Business Writing:** The specialized topics discussed here include appropriate use of acronyms and abbreviations, quotation and citation standards and the use of appendices.

- **Part 5: Refining Your Draft:** The final stage in the writing process is editing and revising. This part of the book offers insights into time-tested editing strategies, the elimination of common errors and the integration of feedback for continuous improvement. It underscores the importance of refining and polishing drafts to achieve clear, concise and effective business writing.

- **Part 6: Using AI in Business Writing:** Generative AI can be useful if employed as a tool and not a crutch, cutting down tremendously on the time it takes to generate a first rough draft of a document. However, it's important to know how to create prompts that will generate worthwhile material and equally important to know how to edit that material.

As you embark on the journey through *Power in Precision*, remember that each part is a stepping stone toward mastering the art of business writing. This book is designed to inform and enhance: it will equip you with the tools to refine your writing, express your ideas more clearly and transform your professional identity. By embracing the principles of precise, clear language, you enhance your ability to influence, persuade and inspire. Let this book be your guide as you seek to elevate your writing and your career. The *Power of Precision* is in your hands; it's time to harness it and unlock new possibilities for your career.

PART

1

Foundations of Effective Writing

In Part 1, we'll first look at how to corral your ideas and organize your thinking, and then we'll talk about techniques for crafting a clear message on the sentence, paragraph and document level.

In Part 1

- Master the art of structured thinking in business writing.
- Craft your message.
- Define your "voice" in business writing.

Master the art of structured thinking in business writing

Embarking on the art of business writing is exciting and daunting. This section is your compass, guiding you from the initial spark of an idea through the meticulous structuring of your thoughts, employing proven frameworks to sharpen your message so it resonates with your intended audience. Whether you're drafting a memo, presenting a strategy or summarizing a complex discussion, the journey to effective writing starts with understanding the core principles that will make your words be remembered.

The initial plunge into writing often poses the greatest challenge. The urge to dive headfirst into the creative waters is strong, yet a methodical approach can significantly amplify the power of your message. Thankfully, there are some strategies to set your writing on a course for success.

> "The scariest moment is always just before you start."
>
> — Stephen King, author

Overcome writer's block with mind maps

Staring at a blank screen or piece of paper can feel akin to trudging through molasses. If you find yourself knowing roughly what to say, but struggling to weave it into a coherent narrative, mind mapping can help. Mind mapping is both a brainstorming tool and a method of visually organizing and prioritizing ideas. It is effective for breaking complex concepts into manageable pieces, and it can help you identify the core themes that will drive your narrative forward.

Mind mapping works best if you use a piece of paper and writing utensil rather than attempt to do it on an electronic device. Imagine you have to write a proposal for an internal company mentorship program. On a large sheet of paper, jot down keywords that encapsulate points that are important to cover. "Goals" will likely be one, and doubtless you will quickly think of subtopics under "goals." "Mentor qualities" might be another category, and you would begin listing qualities that the company wants in mentors, such as seniority, broad experience, patience, interest in working with younger colleagues and so on. As you begin to accumulate keywords and subtopics, notice which ones share aspects with other ones. If, under "mentor qualities," you find you have a number of characteristics related to social skills, then circle all of those. For example, "patience," "interest in working with younger colleagues," "a sense of humor" and "open-mindedness" might all be in that circle, warranting a standalone topic. Should you discover a misplaced idea, simply draw a line to the more appropriate cluster.

This visual exercise clarifies your thoughts and unveils missing pieces of your narrative puzzle. Once you have a good number of ideas and supporting ideas on your paper, you can think about how they should be ordered. In this manner, a storyline emerges from the chaos. For those who find the one-page constraint stifling, Post-it notes offer a dynamic alternative. Arrange and rearrange these sticky notes to play with your initial ideas. (You can perform this brainstorming in your favorite writing application on your tablet or laptop, but you may find the tactile nature of writing and moving words or Post-its around feels more immersive and stimulates your creative thinking in a more unconstrained, fulfilling way.)

Structure your thinking using Minto's Pyramid Principle

If you're having trouble figuring out how to order your ideas, Barbara Minto's *The Pyramid Principle* can help. Written by business consultant Barbara Minto, the first woman to be hired by the prestigious McKinsey & Company consulting firm, *The Pyramid Principle* is highly regarded and widely used throughout the business world. It recommends starting with your core message, supporting it with grouped arguments and detailing each with evidence. This approach makes complex information digestible and persuasive, and your audience will be able to grasp the essence of your message without getting lost in details.

Organize your thinking around your main idea

Start by asking, what is your main idea? Let's move from mentorship to a new example. Let's imagine you're writing a blog post on AI, and your main idea is that AI can enhance business writing.

The initial notes you brainstormed should give you points that support your main idea. For each point, list your supporting evidence. It will form a pyramid with the evidence for each supporting point at the base, then those supporting ideas and then the main idea at the pinnacle. As you move your points around, identify and fill gaps in your thinking. Refrain, however, from expanding this outline into paragraphs at this stage. Brevity is your ally.

A simplified outline for your blog post on AI in business writing might look like this:

Main idea: AI can enhance business writing.

- **Efficiency:** AI tools can speed up the writing process.
  - **Evidence:** AI-powered tools like Grammarly for grammar correction or Zapier for automating routine content management tasks reduce time spent on those tasks.
- **Creativity:** AI generates ideas for new content.
  - **Evidence:** AI programs such as OpenAI's GPT can generate creative writing prompts or even draft articles based on keywords.
- **Accuracy:** AI enhances fact-checking.
  - **Evidence**: Tools like Turnitin check for plagiarism and accuracy in citations.

"Have a point. It makes it so much more interesting for the listener."

— Neal Page in *Planes, Trains and Automobiles* (1987)

Check for exclusivity and exhaustiveness

Minto teaches that your supporting evidence for your main idea should be mutually exclusive and collectively exhaustive (MECE). Applying the MECE test helps confirm your analysis is thorough and organized, which is critical for making compelling arguments in business writing. Let's look at the two components of the MECE test:

- **Mutually exclusive (ME):** This means that each supporting idea stands alone with no overlap with any other supporting idea. Making sure your supporting ideas are mutually exclusive promotes clear distinctions between pieces of information.

- **Collectively exhaustive (CE):** This means that all possible supporting ideas are covered, leaving no aspect of the main idea unaddressed.

You can use the MECE test to assess your pyramid. Does the evidence for each of your supporting ideas belong clearly to one, and only one, category? Are the supporting ideas themselves unique and mutually exclusive? Focusing on exclusivity eliminates ambiguity and overlap, streamlining analysis and decision making. Have your supporting ideas, taken together, encompassed all possible items or points of consideration, leaving no stone unturned? This comprehensiveness means nothing is overlooked in your evaluation.

To validate that the blog post on AI in business writing passes the MECE test, ask: Do efficiency, creativity and accuracy represent all the ways AI can improve business writing without overlapping? Is there any way in which AI enhances business writing not captured by these categories?

The MECE test is a powerful tool for checking your message's clarity and precision. However, it demands an acute awareness of potential pitfalls:

- **Distinction:** It's crucial that your categories (your supporting points) are clearly defined to prevent any overlap, allowing each idea to contribute distinctly to your argument.

- **Full coverage:** Regularly reassess whether your categories comprehensively cover all relevant aspects of your main idea. Collaborative brainstorming sessions are invaluable for uncovering overlooked details that will enrich your narrative.

- **Forgo the "other" category:** For precision in analysis, avoid lumping disparate ideas into an "other" category. Each piece of information should be thoughtfully categorized to maintain the integrity of your argument.

Use Minto's situation-complication-resolution (SCR) framework to further your understanding

Many business writing projects involve identifying challenges and proposing solutions, and for those tasks, Minto's situation-complication-resolution (SCR) framework is an indispensable tool.

The SCR framework simplifies complex narratives by defining the context (situation), outlining the challenges (complication) and presenting a solution or solutions (resolution). This structuring is vital for crafting compelling business stories that align with strategic goals and resonate with the intended audience.

Not all business writing involves proposing a solution to a problem. Sometimes you may just be presenting findings, for instance. Attempting to force all types of writing into an SCR format can confuse the point or create artificial urgency. However, sometimes even when your writing project doesn't appear suited to an SCR presentation, it can benefit from its structured process. Take our blog post on AI in business writing. Our main point is that AI can enhance business writing, and then we back that point up with our evidence. In this case our main point involves a situation (writing in a business setting) with an implied complication: business writing is difficult and time consuming. We can fruitfully apply the SCR framework:

- **Situation:** Establish the current state of business writing. For instance, acknowledge the existing challenges in business writing, such as time constraints and the demand for high-quality content.

  Example: *"XYZ Corporation, a leading firm in the technology industry, faced significant challenges in maintaining a steady flow of high-quality, innovative and error-free business communications. The increasing demand for engaging content and need for efficiency in content production posed a substantial hurdle."*

- **Complication:** Highlight the problem or challenge. In our example, the increasing need for efficiency and innovation in business writing presents a significant hurdle.

  Example: *"The primary challenges included a high rate of grammatical errors, which compromised the professionalism of communications. Inefficiencies in content production processes hindered the team's ability to focus on strategic and creative tasks. Without innovative content, XYZ Corporation failed to engage its target audience effectively."*

- **Resolution:** Show how AI offers a solution by automating tasks, fostering creativity and delivering accuracy. Taken together, these improvements can be presented as driving significant beneficial changes.

  Example: *"To overcome these challenges, XYZ Corporation strategically integrated a suite of AI tools tailored to its specific needs. Grammarly was employed for real-time grammar correction, Zapier for streamlining content workflow and OpenAI's GPT for generating creative content ideas. This integration resulted in a 30% increase in content production efficiency, allowing the team to allocate more time to strategy and creativity. There was a 50% reduction in grammatical errors, significantly elevating the professionalism of their communications. Furthermore, a 25% uplift in audience engagement was observed, demonstrating the value of innovative and accurately tailored communications."*

In moving to an SCR structure, detailed statistics on AI tool efficiencies or in-depth examples of creative content generation may be relegated to supporting documentation. This means the narrative remains focused and powerful, while supplementary details are accessible for those interested in a deeper dive.

From SCR to RSC

Depending on your needs and the needs of your audience, the components of the SCR framework can rearranged for an alternative resolution-situation-complication (RSC) format. For instance, when addressing a time-constrained executive audience, leading with the resolution—the actionable insights or solutions—captures attention and sets the tone for the importance of the subsequent information. Knowing to make this switch demonstrates a strong grasp on effective communication.

If we decided to use an RCS format for our AI example, we might start with the transformative effect of AI tools, highlighting that Grammarly and OpenAI's GPT can revolutionize business writing, enhancing both efficiency and accuracy. We would then detail the current challenges—inefficiency and frequent errors—and conclude by situating these issues within the broader context of evolving business communication needs.

Challenges with the SCR (or RSC) Framework

When transitioning from the outlining and planning phase to the actual writing phase, it's crucial to understand not every idea generated in the mind map or outlined in the pyramid will make it into the final draft. This selection process is where strategic thinking and audience awareness come into play. You curate the content to include only the most relevant information for your specific audience.

But be careful in trimming the resolution. A well-defined resolution should include specifics about what needs to be done, how it should be implemented, by whom and within what time frame. This level of detail is crucial for actionable writing because it moves the narrative from suggestions to a clear road map for implementation. For instance, if the resolution involves adopting AI tools to improve business writing, specify which tools could be used, how they will enhance efficiency, creativity and accuracy, who within the organization should lead the initiative and a timeline for adoption and evaluation.

Methodical planning is worth the investment. Jumping straight into writing may be energizing, but without thoughtful structure and curation of ideas and evidence, you will inevitably face considerable challenges and frustrations when it comes to editing. Mind maps and Minto's tools are valuable ways to structure your approach.

Craft your message

Now that you have a solid foundation in structuring ideas and organizing thoughts, the journey progresses to the tangible act of writing. It's time to flesh out these bare-bones ideas into full-bodied narratives that resonate and compel action. This section empowers you to do that, but we'll take it one step at a time. Eventually, your writing needs to be precise, concise and compelling. But not at the start. Right now you need to relax and let words flow. The following strategies can kickstart your writing process.

Guidance on initiating the writing process

Strategy	Guidance
Embrace spontaneity in drafting	Dive into writing with the freedom to express ideas fluidly, without immediate concern for perfect grammar or the ideal word. This approach encourages a rich flow of ideas, fostering creativity and originality right from the start.
Use versatile notetaking strategies	Embrace traditional and digital methods for capturing ideas on the fly, whether it's jotting down on paper, sticky notes or using apps. This approach means you're always ready to capture inspiration.
Resist premature editing	Focus on getting the bulk of your words and ideas into your initial drafts. Early-stage editing will hinder the creative process, so save meticulous revisions for later in your writing process.
Create a "parking lot" for divergent ideas	Use a system for sidelining interesting but currently unrelated ideas—a "parking lot" where these thoughts can be parked for potential future exploration.

Pay special attention to beginnings and endings

Later in this section we'll work on tailoring your writing for particular audiences and types of communication, but two elements of the writing process are universally important, regardless of the audience or writing task. These are your beginning and your ending—your beginning because it's with your title and first few sentences that you will either hook your readers or lose them, and your ending because that's where you are sharing your most important takeaways. Let's spend some time with titles, beginnings and endings.

Select compelling titles to grab attention

A quick note before we dive in: although the title is the first thing your readers will see, it often will be the last thing that you write because you need a sense of your completed project in order to craft the perfect title. Trying to select a title before you have finished your writing can be a great waste of time, so although we're covering it first, save creating it for last.

The power of a well-crafted title cannot be overstated. Yet selecting a compelling title is an art form. It is important to know what works and doesn't.

Guidance on selecting compelling titles

Advice	Explanation
Avoid clichés, but use originality with care	Steer clear of overused phrases like "Game-Changer," "Cutting-Edge Solutions," or "Navigating Stormy Waters." Keep in mind that although creativity can enhance a title, you must be sure it is easy to understand.
Be clear and precise	Your title should shine a light on your core message in a succinct manner. It's the first opportunity to make an impression—make it count by being direct and unambiguous.
Offer a value proposition	Your title should make a promise, hinting at the insights, guidance or solutions the reader will gain. It should accurately reflect the content's value, avoiding hyperbole to maintain trust and credibility.

Some examples of possible title styles follow in the table below.

Styles of titles for different types of writing

Style	Example
Case studies	"How Company X Succeeded in a Competitive Market" indicates that it will offer real-life examples of practical strategies.
Challenges and solutions	"Overcoming Supply Chain Disruptions in Global Markets" indicates what problems it addresses and hints at solutions, encouraging readers seeking answers.
Direct benefits	"Boost Your Sales with These Proven Techniques" speaks directly to the reader, promising tangible improvements.
Future predictions	"The Future of Remote Work: Trends to Watch in 2025" intrigues readers with the promise of forecasts about relevant topics.

Style	Example
How-to guides	"How to Drive Innovation in Your Team" indicates that it will provide practical tips in a straightforward format.
Listicles	"Five Time-Saving Strategies for Busy Executives" is in the classic listicle format: it says how many points will be covered and promises clear, actionable advice that appeals to a specific audience.
Myth busting	"Debunking Common Myths about Digital Marketing" appeals by promising to correct misconceptions.
Personalization	"Managing Your Work-Life Balance: A Guide for Parents" speaks directly to a specific group's challenges.
Provocative statements	"The Biggest Mistakes Managers Don't Know They're Making" grabs attention by injecting unease in the target readership, who will want to be sure they are not making these mistakes.
Questions	"What Can We Learn from the Latest Market Trends?" engages readers by posing a question they want answered.
Statistics and data	"75% of Start-Ups Fail: Here's How to Be in the 25%" uses attention-grabbing numbers to draw in readers looking for factual insights.

Use powerful introductions to engage readers from the start

A compelling introduction draws readers in and provides a clear idea of what they can expect. Aim to keep the introduction brief, and make each sentence add value and directly relate to the content that follows.

Guidance on writing compelling introductions

Recommendation	Explanation
Engage from the start	Begin with a statement or question that is relevant, intriguing and rooted in reality to instantly grab the reader's attention.
Convey uniqueness	Highlight what sets your content apart from other writing on the same topic through a distinct perspective, new research findings or an unconventional approach.
Define scope	Clearly articulate the aim of your content, setting realistic expectations (do not overpromise) to clarify focus and pique interest.
Establish context and relevance	Briefly explain the current importance of the topic, linking it to broader industry or global trends to emphasize significance and relevance.
Include a compelling statistic or fact	Including a surprising or significant statistic or fact will capture attention and underscore the topic's importance.
Preview key points	Subtly hint at the main points your content will explore or the conclusions you will reach, setting the stage for readers and encouraging them to read on for details.

Quick-take bullets can be an effective way to summarize key points or findings right at the beginning, providing readers with a snapshot of your content's value. Aim for three to five bullets to keep the overview manageable and readable. Each bullet should be concise, ideally one sentence long, and highlight a main point or insight that will be explored in greater detail in the content. The reader may stop here, if they are in a hurry, so each bullet should offer a real insight or value proposition that both provides them with something of value right away and encourages them to read on for the full context or analysis. Steer clear of simply stating "this report covers"; your title and introduction should already convey that.

Craft purposeful endings to leave a lasting impression

A well-crafted conclusion serves as the capstone of your document, offering a moment to summarize key insights, ponder broader implications and, where appropriate, spur the reader into action. Its presentation can vary depending on the document's purpose and structure.

Guidance on writing compelling conclusions

Element	Description	Example
Action or exploration	Conclude with a call to action or a question that promotes further thought, investigation or engagement.	"Adopting these practices could transform customer trust and loyalty in the digital age."
Broader implications	Explore what the findings or arguments mean for the future, industry or reader's context, adding depth to the analysis.	"These developments suggest a significant shift in consumer preferences toward privacy-focused applications."
Practical tips	Offer practical tips or steps that readers can take in response to the information presented, making the conclusion action oriented.	"To start, regularly update and review digital security protocols."
Quote from thought leaders	Ending with a powerful quote from a thought leader in the field can lend authority to your conclusion and inspire readers.	"As Jan Jansen once said, 'Embracing digital transformation is not just an option but a necessity for securing a competitive edge.'"
Reflective Insights	Incorporate insights that encourage readers to reflect on how the information affects their views or actions, making the conclusion more personal and introspective.	"Consider how integrating these insights could alter your approach to digital marketing strategies."
Summary of insights	Recap the document's main points with clarity, emphasizing the core message succinctly.	"Through our analysis, we've identified key strategies for enhancing digital security."
Visual summary	Consider including a visual summary, such as an infographic, in the conclusion to reinforce key points visually for those who absorb information better this way.	[An infographic summarizing the key strategies for enhancing digital security.]

It's important to bring your writing neatly to a close, but concluding a document effectively doesn't always require a formal "In Conclusion" section. For brief memos or documents rich in tips and recommendations, a succinct closing statement or a call to action often suffices. For documents with conclusion sections, titles like "Next Steps" or "Looking Ahead" suggest forward momentum that encourages reader engagement.

Craft effective sentences and paragraphs

The ability to express your ideas in coherent sentences and paragraphs is central to powerful writing. Through clear and varied sentence structures and sensibly constructed paragraphs, you will guide your reader through your thoughts with ease.

"The hardest thing about writing is writing."

— Nora Ephron, journalist, author and filmmaker

Master sentence structure to keep the reader engaged

Words alone can't tell a story, issue a warning or recommend a course of action. It's at the sentence level that meaning and import begin to come into focus. For this reason, it's important to master effective sentence construction.

Avoid sentence fragments

First and foremost, you want to be sure your sentences are complete. Sentence fragments often will sneak into writing when people are trying to be concise or dramatic, but unfortunately they end up muddling the message. Always write complete sentences that convey your points effectively and leave no room for misinterpretation. A complete sentence will have a subject (the main actor— sometimes only implied) and an action or state that the subject does or is in. A fragment often lacks both.

Examples of sentence fragments and suggestions for completing them

Sentence fragment	Explanation	Complete sentence	Explanation
After the meeting about budget cuts.	This fragment lacks both a subject and an action or state for the subject to do or be in.	After the meeting about budget cuts, the department heads devised a new strategy.	This complete sentence has both a subject (the department heads) and an action they are doing (devising a new strategy).
The new marketing plan for next quarter.	This fragment has a possible subject (the new marketing plan) but no action the subject is taking or state that the subject is in.	The new marketing plan for next quarter has three key elements.	The addition of "has three key elements" provides the state that the new marketing plan is in, which makes this a complete sentence.
To try to improve team productivity.	This fragment lacks both a subject and an action or state for the subject to do or be in.	The manager introduced new software to try to improve team productivity.	This complete sentence has both a subject (the manager) and an action the subject is doing (introducing new software).

Vary length and complexity in your sentences

To maintain readers' interest, it's good to have sentences of varying length and complexity. Aim to express your ideas in a way that is easily understandable, avoiding unnecessary jargon and complex language. Below are some examples.

Guidance on writing well-crafted sentences

Strategy	Description	Example	Explanation
Vary sentence length	Rather than a succession of short, staccato sentences, include some sentences that are longer and more complex. This technique adds dynamism to your writing.	**Before:** "Our team is equipped to tackle challenges. We anticipate challenges. The challenges will be met with innovative solutions." **After:** "While we anticipate challenges, our team is equipped to tackle them with innovative solutions."	Three short, simple sentences have been combined to create a longer, more complex sentence. The goal is not to make all your sentences complex but rather to vary them.
Clarify with specific terminology	Replace vague language with specific details to clarify and strengthen your message.	**Before:** "We will address the issue soon." **After:** "We will address the issue by the end of the week."	A nonspecific time (soon) has been replaced with a specific time frame (the end of the week).
Cut unnecessary words for conciseness	Enhance clarity and dynamism by omitting repetitive phrases or information that can be intuited from the context. This technique makes your writing crisper and more engaging.	**Before:** "The first quarter saw an increase in sales. The second quarter saw a decrease in sales." **After:** "The first quarter saw an increase in sales; the second, a decrease."	The two sentences have been combined, which allows for the removal of the words "quarter" and "in sales," both of which are clear from context.
Integrate questions sparingly	Use questions to provoke thought or emphasize a point, but use them sparingly to maintain the authoritative tone of your writing.	**Before:** "We need to reconsider our strategy and think about how we will adapt to these changes. We need to consider what our next steps should be." **After:** "In light of these changes, how will we adapt our strategy? What steps should we take next?"	Sentences that stated the situation have been replaced by sentences that induce the reader to ask questions about the situation.
Use the power of three	Grouping concepts or adjectives in threes can make your writing more memorable and persuasive. Be sure, however, hat the three things you mention are genuinely distinct—don't simply repeat one concept with three different words.	**Before:** "Our solution is efficient and convenient. It is also economical." **After:** "Our solution is efficient, convenient and economical."	The three qualities of the solution now form in an easy-to-remember string.

Strategy	Description	Example	Explanation
Vary sentence openers	Avoid starting consecutive sentences with the same word or phrase. Variety in sentence openers keeps the reader engaged.	**Before:** "The manager announced the new strategy. The manager convened a meeting immediately afterward. The manager outlined the implementation phases." **After:** "The manager announced the new strategy. Immediately afterward, she convened a meeting in which she outlined the implementation phases."	The sentences no longer all start with "the manager," and the result flows better, sounds more professional and s likely to be more engaging to readers.

Beyond this general advice, there are several additional points to keep in mind as you write more powerful sentences as the foundation for your writing:

Select the right article ("a"/"an," "the"), depending on whether you're being general or specific

As you write, remember that articles specify whether you're referring to something particular ("the") or general ("a"/"an"). "The book" refers to a particular book. In your writing, you would use "the book" to speak about a book that you had referred to earlier. "A book" refers to any possible book. In your writing, you would use "a book" if you were speaking generally or making a general example. When referring to specific items or entities that are already known to the reader or that have been previously mentioned, opt for "the." When referring to something in general, opt for "a"/"an" ("a" before words that start with a consonant sound, and "an" before words that start with a vowel sound).

- **General:** "**A** manager must communicate clearly." (Indicates any manager, not a particular manager.)
- **Specific:** "**The** manager of our department communicates clearly." (Refers to a specific manager.)

Avoid starting sentences with "it"

While using "it" to start your sentences can streamline them and prevent redundancy, sometimes it can introduce ambiguity if it's not clear what "it" refers to. In passive sentence constructions ("It has been learned…" "It is often said…" "It was announced…") "it" hides the subject, reducing clarity, which can frustrate readers.

When you begin a sentence with "it," check that the reader can readily discern what "It" refers to. If the preceding sentences make that clear, then using "It" can help avoid unnecessary repetition. However, if there is any uncertainty, consider revising the sentence to explicitly state the subject of the action.

In this example, the "it" has a clear referent, so it's fine to use it.

- "The company had a successful quarter. **It** is now on track to exceed its annual revenue record." (Here, "It" clearly refers to "the company.")

In this example, the "it" is unclear, and the sentence needs to be reworded.

- **Before:** "The buzz on Wall Street was that the Fed would lower interest rates and that SpaceX would go public. **It** did not, however." (Here it is unclear whether "it" refers to the Fed lowering interest rates or SpaceX going public.)
- **After:** "The buzz on Wall Street was that the Fed would lower interest rates and that SpaceX would go public. The first turned out to be true but not the second." (Now it is clear which of the two things did not happen.)

End sentences with the key points

When presenting information, it's good to keep in mind the recency effect—namely, that the last items presented in a series will be the best remembered. By judiciously ending sentences with key points, you increase the likelihood that your audience will remember them.

- **Original:** "The company achieved its **most successful quarter** in terms of revenue this year."
- **Adapted:** "The company's revenue reached **an all-time high this quarter**."

Be selective in placing prepositions (e.g., "in," "by," "at" or "from") at the end of sentences

It's completely natural in speech to end a sentence in a preposition. Moreover, great thinkers such as Susan B. Anthony, Charles Darwin and John Stuart Mill all used sentences that end in prepositions in their writings. However, as the Churchill quote highlights, you may encounter colleagues or superiors who take you to task if you end a sentence with one. There's little merit in engaging in frivolous debate, so be pragmatic: in formal documents, if you can express the same meaning clearly without ending the sentence in a preposition, you will protect yourself against self-inflicted criticism. (For emails and informal communications, don't trouble yourself, just write it how you'd say it.)

"A preposition is a terrible thing to end a sentence with."

— Attributed to Winston S. Churchill, former UK prime minister, military officer and writer

---

Examples of ways to rephrase a sentence to avoid a preposition at the end:

- **Before:** "This is the platform we collaborate **on**."
- **After:** "This platform is where our collaboration takes place."
- **Before:** "What are the main challenges you are dealing **with**?"
- **After:** "What challenges are you currently facing?"
- **Before:** "Who should the report be submitted **to**?"
- **After:** "To whom should the report be submitted?"

Focus on clear paragraph structure

Now that you understand the principles of a good sentence, let's move on to the next unit of thought: the paragraph.

Paragraph structure is key to conveying complex information with clarity. Each paragraph should be a cogent unit of thought, introduced by a **clear topic sentence** that sets the stage for what follows. This sentence should succinctly introduce the main idea of the paragraph, serving as a signpost for readers. It establishes the context and direction, guiding the subsequent sentences.

Follow the topic sentence with **supporting sentences**. These sentences elaborate on the main idea, providing details, examples or explanations. They build on the topic sentence, adding depth and nuance to your argument or narrative.

Maintain focus on your paragraphs. This means keeping each paragraph focused on a single idea. Mixing multiple ideas can confuse readers and dilute the effect of your message. If a new idea emerges, it deserves its own paragraph.

End your paragraph with a **concluding or transition sentence**. A concluding sentence wraps up the paragraph's main idea with a summary statement or draws a conclusion from the paragraph's content, while a transition sentence provides a link to the topic of the next paragraph.

A paragraph should be easy to read and understand. Avoid overly long sentences or complex jargon that could alienate readers. Read paragraphs aloud and put yourself in the reader's shoes: if you're out of breath or confused by the time you finish the paragraph, it is not well written. Try again.

Below is an example of a paragraph before and after applying effective writing techniques.

Guidance on structuring powerful paragraphs

Disorganized paragraph	Reorganized paragraph
In our efforts to expand, we've entered new markets and added to our product line in the last few years. The new markets are Cambodia, Vietnam and the Philippines, and the new products are frozen ice cream bars, sorbets and frozen yogurts. We have exited Brunei, however. The company website has been refreshed. Sorbet sales are especially noteworthy. Despite production issues in Vietnam, sales in all the new markets have been very strong.	In our efforts to expand, we've entered new markets in Southeast Asia (Cambodia, Vietnam and the Philippines) and added exciting new products: frozen ice cream bars, sorbets and frozen yogurts. Despite production issues in Vietnam, sales in all the new markets have been very strong, with sorbet sales being especially noteworthy.

Explanation: The original paragraph presented information about the new markets and new products in a jumbled fashion. Readers would have a hard time following the train of thought and might miss salient information. The paragraph also included information about the exit from Brunei, which is not relevant in a paragraph on entering new markets. The sentence about the company website is irrelevant, although it could be added back in at the end of the paragraph if it was reworded to reflect the changes the company has undergone (e.g., "The company website has been refreshed to reflect these changes."). The revised paragraph presents the information in a coherent fashion: first the new markets, then the new products, then the results of these changes.

Define your "voice" in business writing

Your voice is the distinct style that makes your writing uniquely yours. Your voice conveys your personality, perspective and values; it's what makes your writing recognizable and relatable.

Be purposeful in defining your voice

In business writing, finding your voice involves balancing your natural writing tendencies with the expectations of your audience and the conventions of the genre. Here are some pointers for developing your voice:

- **Be authentic:** Write from your experience and knowledge; don't try to adopt the standpoint or persona of someone else. Authenticity resonates. Remember, though, that authenticity comes into play only after you've mastered the basic guidelines for writing good sentences, paragraphs and complete reports. The danger with bringing in your authentic voice is you forgo the precision required in powerful writing.

- **Be observant:** Learn from others. Pay close attention to the style and voice used across different formats. Consider studying articles from reputable sources such as *The Economist*,

Harvard Business Review and *McKinsey Quarterly*. These publications are exemplary in the field of business writing. Observe how they skillfully employ prose and visuals to engage, inform and persuade their audience. Try to incorporate similar strategies into your own writing to improve its effectiveness.

■ **Be reflective:** Regularly review your writing to identify what works and what doesn't. Reflect on feedback and be willing to let your voice evolve over time.

■ **Be flexible:** Your voice shouldn't be a rigid thing. It can and should adapt to different contexts. For example, you will take a more relaxed tone in an email communication to a colleague than you will when writing a white paper.

To further explore and refine your unique voice in business writing, consider these exercises:

■ **Reflect on the phrases or terms that resonate with you personally.** Do certain words or narrative styles draw you in more than others?

■ **Think about how you would explain a complex business strategy to a friend.** The language, analogies and examples you naturally gravitate toward can reveal much about your authentic voice. Such introspection aids in identifying your natural style.

A well-defined voice will make your work more engaging and help build your personal or corporate brand. By thoughtfully applying creativity and tailoring your voice to different contexts, you can elevate your business writing from merely informative to truly influential.

Adapt your style and voice to the context

Creativity in business writing doesn't mean sacrificing clarity for flair; it means knowing how to adapt your message to engage your audience effectively, regardless of the medium. Whether crafting a thought leadership piece, devising a marketing strategy or communicating with senior executives, the infusion of creativity should always aim to enhance understanding and engagement. You should modulate the level of creativity and expression in your voice to suit the format and purpose of your document.

Your writing will likely fall into one of the following three categories:

■ **Engagement writing:** This allows for a more casual and conversational tone.
  ○ **Example:** "Let's talk about customer service—it's the secret sauce behind every winning business, turning satisfied customers into loyal fans and chatterboxes about your brand."

A good way to engage the reader is to include relatable stories or intriguing insights. These will make your content shareable and discussion-worthy.

■ **Informative writing:** Aim for clarity and precision. Your voice should be authoritative but accessible, delivering information without unnecessary complexity. Consistency is essential; don't try to add panache by changing terminology.
  ○ **Example:** "This month, sales increased by 15% due to effective marketing strategies and the introduction of new product lines."

■ **Persuasive writing:** Here, you want to use emotional appeal and strong arguments to convince the reader of your proposition or conclusion. Creativity can be used to craft compelling narratives that underscore your message.
  ○ **Example**: "Now is not the time to be timid: we must seize the opportunity offered by novel digital marketing strategies to achieve an additional 25 percent growth in sales."

The guidance below offers a more fine-grained look at tailoring your writing to specific tasks.

Guidance on tailoring your voice to the medium

Document type	Guidance
Corporate documents	Precision and consistency are key. Use clear, direct language to convey policies and procedures. The goal is to have the audience understand and act on the information without room for misinterpretation. Use consistent wording throughout.
Customer correspondence	Personalization and empathy can enhance communication with customers. Your voice should be supportive and understanding, focusing on addressing the customer's needs and concerns.
Executive summaries and reports	Aim for clarity and conciseness, using creativity to make data and insights engaging without compromising their seriousness. Your voice should be authoritative, focusing on conveying complex information in an accessible manner.
Internal communications	A conversational tone can make communications like memos and newsletters more relatable. Your voice should be inclusive, fostering a sense of community and shared purpose.
Marketing content	You can include emotion in your marketing writing. You are aiming to create a good impression of the brand among your readers, one that will boost their loyalty and induce them to take the actions (purchase, word-of-mouth evangelism) you desire.
Thought leadership articles	With thought leadership articles, you will be introducing and exploring ideas. You want to focus on good organization, clarity and meaningful examples so that readers can understand all the facets of the ideas you are sharing.
Training and instructional materials	To write good instructional materials, you need to be able to simplify complex concepts and express procedures in ways that are easy to understand. Clever visuals or examples can help make learning engaging, but clarity is most important.

Effective business communication requires an understanding of the diverse contexts in which your writing will be encountered. It's important to align your writing style with the intended purpose, so your message resonates with your audience and achieves its desired effect. The most effective business communicators are those who remain curious and committed to authentic expression.

Use editing to improve your writing

Editing is an important part of the writing process. Whether you edit yourself, reading over your own work to catch errors and make improvements, or whether colleagues or others offer you that service, editing helps you polish your work and clarify your message. When others read a draft of your work and offer comments, you have the opportunity to reflect on their feedback. You can come to see patterns in your writing that may need improvement. Each iteration is a learning opportunity. Embracing editing as an integral part of your writing process encourages significant improvements and growth. We'll look more closely at the transformative power of editing in Part 5.

* * * * *

Now that you have learned how to organize your ideas, what basic sentence and paragraph structure is and the importance of developing your own distinct voice, it is time to turn to some advanced writing techniques that will take your writing to a new level of precision and power.

PART

2

Advanced Writing Techniques

Part 2 focuses on mastering some of the more tricky aspects of writing, such as complicated verb tenses, the active and passive voice, how the parts of a sentence work together, choosing the right words and avoiding jargon and excess verbiage so your writing shines.

In Part 2

- Understand the power of verbs in all their tenses and moods.
- Choose between active and passive voice to bring energy and focus.
- Make sure the parts of your sentence interact harmoniously.
- Use connecting and transition words properly.
- Balance formality and conversational tone when using contracted words.
- Use punctuation correctly.
- Use advanced punctuation and styling for emphasis and engagement.
- Embrace positive phrasing.
- Write in an inclusive and respectful style.
- Use direct, accessible language.
- Be succinct.

Understand the power of verbs in all their tenses and moods

More than any other part of speech, verbs are what bring writing to life. In this section, you'll learn to choose the verb tense (past, present or future) that suits your needs, along with the dangers of overreliance on phrases that start with present participles ("-ing" words). This section also touches on the subjunctive mood and covers modal verbs (which tell us what we **must** or **should** do), the advantages of strong verbs over adverbs and choosing the correct verbs for your purposes.

Choose the right tense

Tense selection situates your audience in the proper time frame. The future tense issues promises and predicts the future. ("The company **will open** a new branch office in February.") The present tense narrates universals and general practice. ("Here at QT Corporation, we **value** our employees' contributions.") The past tense describes things that happened in the past. ("During the Great Recession, we **retrenched**.")

The past tense can be especially difficult because different levels of past can be expressed by adding "have/has" and "had." "I went home," "I have gone home" and "I had gone home" all mean something different.

- **I went home** is a statement about the past.
- **I have gone home** is a statement about the present, describing a past event.
- **I had gone home** is a statement about a past that happened before some other event that's in the more recent past (e.g., "I had gone home before I heard the news.").

Consistency in tense presentation helps readers understand the order of events in your writing, while inconsistency can lead to confusion about what happened when.

"The past, the present, and the future walked into a bar. It was tense."

— Lex Martin, author

Examples of inconsistent tense

Inconsistent tense	Consistent tense	Explanation
The team **planned** a new product and **has presented** it last week.	The team **planned** a new product and **presented** it last week.	The sentence is describing events and situations in the past, with no reference to the present, so "has" needs to be deleted.
The manager **reviews** the quarterly report and **decided** to adjust the budget allocations.	The manager **reviewed** the quarterly report and **decided** to adjust the budget allocations.	"The manager reviews…" is a statement about general practice, but here we're talking about one particular review in the past that led to the manager's decision. For that reason, we need "reviewed" (past tense).
Our company **powers** its offices with on-site solar panels, and every year it **received** sustainability awards.	Our company **powers** its offices with on-site solar panels, and every year it **receives** sustainability awards.	Here, the sentence is describing an ongoing reality, so the present tense is needed for both verbs.

Know when to say "I were" and "it were"

The past tense of "I am" is "I was." So why do we hear the phrase "If I were you," and is it correct?

"If I were you" and equivalent sentences that start "If he were… " or "If it were…" are indeed correct. They are practically the only place in English where you encounter special grammar for expressing the verb "mood" called the subjunctive. This mood is used for hypothetical and contrary-to-fact situations. For the purposes of business writing, the easiest thing to remember is that if a sentence starts with "If I…," "if she/he…" or "if it…" then use "were," not "was":

- **"If she were** boss, the workday would start at 10 a.m." (She is not the boss.)
- **"If it were** left to chance, it would never get done." (It is not left to chance.)
- **"When I was** the manager, I ordered lunch for the office once a week." (This is not hypothetical; I was the manager and am describing something that really happened, so "was" is appropriate.)

Note: British English does not use the subjunctive mood as much as American English. See Appendix 2 for more detail.

Avoid phrases that start with present participles ("ing" words)

Present participles (the "-ing" form of verbs: running, thinking, singing, etc.) can give a sense of immediacy, of something that is happening right now. But too many present participles can overwhelm a sentence or make for a sing-song quality.

Consider the goal of your sentence. Is the action you're describing ongoing? Perhaps you want to highlight that two or more actions are happening at the same time, or you want to set the scene or provide background information that is continuous in nature. In those cases, present participles convey this effectively. When your goal is to describe actions or intentions in a straightforward manner without the need for expressing continuity or simultaneity, simply state clear, direct actions or intentions using a simple verb form.

Guidance on deciding whether or not to use a present participle:

■ **Before:** "**Having** meetings **running** over time is **causing** delays in project completion."

■ **After:** "Meetings **running** over time cause project delays." (The revision simplifies the sentence, clearly linking overlong meetings directly to project delays without too much repetition of the present participle verb form.)

■ **Before:** "By **implementing** changes and **making** adjustments, we are **seeing** improvements in productivity."

■ **After:** "**Implementing** changes and **adjusting** processes have improved our productivity." (This simplification removes the continuous aspect with regard to the outcome, resulting in a more concise sentence.)

Use modal verbs (e.g., "must," "should") to convey certainty and possibility

Modal verbs, always used with other verbs, are how we express that something is possible, necessary or obligatory. Writers often overlook the significant effect choosing the appropriate modal verb can have on the definitiveness of a recommendation or conclusion. For instance, "must" and "should" create a significantly different tone and will alter your message accordingly. Careful selection of your modal verbs will make your most important recommendations or perspectives stand out from the less important ones.

Modal verbs ranked from the most to the least in terms of obligation or necessity

Verb	Tone	Example
Shall	Formal obligation or future action	"The company **shall** disclose any breaches immediately."
Must	Obligation, necessity or logical conclusion	"All team members **must** complete the training by next Friday."
Should	Recommendation or advice, often with an implication of duty or expectation	"Companies **should** regularly update their cybersecurity policies."
Could	Possibility or polite suggestion	"You **could** streamline the process by adopting new software."
Would	Conditional or polite intention	"We **would** like to propose a new strategy."

It is important to appreciate that choice of "**may**" or "**might**" can subtly shift the nuance of possibility or permission in your sentences. "May" is often used to express a higher degree of likelihood or to formally grant permission: "You may leave early if you finish your work." It carries a sense of present or future possibility that's more immediate or likely. "Might" suggests a lower probability, a finer shade of speculation about events that are less certain: "I might go to the party if I have time." It's the choice for expressing tentative plans or uncertain outcomes, especially in hypothetical or speculative situations.

Choose active verbs over adverbs

Effective writing captivates readers with its momentum and vitality. Unfortunately, writers often weaken the momentum of their writing through excessive use of adverbs (words that modify verbs, adjectives or other adverbs). Before you do so, first ask, Is the adverb necessary? Or can it be removed? (see "Eliminate superfluous modifiers (e.g., 'generally')," below, for more advice). If you want an adverb to convey additional insight, ask yourself whether a stronger, more dynamic verb could supplant a weaker verb-adverb pairing. Just be sure, before you make the switch, that the meaning of your replacement verb fully captures the meaning you were seeking to convey with your originally pairing.

- **Before:** "She **quickly ran** to the meeting."
- **After:** "She **sprinted** to the meeting." (Using a more precise verb eliminates the need for an adverb, enhancing the sentence.)
- **Before:** "The project was **very slowly** moving toward completion."
- **After:** "The project **crawled** toward completion." (A vivid verb choice provides a clearer, more immediate understanding of the project's pace.)

"Write with nouns and verbs, not with adjectives and adverbs. The adjective hasn't been built that can pull a weak or inaccurate noun out of a tight place."

— E. B. White, author

Split infinitives strategically, not routinely

The splitting of infinitives—the placing of an adverb between "to" and a verb—is one of those topics, like ending a sentence in a preposition, that brings can irk readers, especially those viewing themselves (often incorrectly) as grammar experts. However, when employed thoughtfully, this technique can enhance your message by injecting urgency, improving tempo and clarifying meaning. Just be conscious of what you're doing and be sure your use is justified and strategic, rather than mere grammatical rebellion. Before finalizing a sentence, read it aloud with the adverb positioned before, within and after the infinitive. Choose the placement that delivers your intended message most effectively.

Examples of wisely chosen split infinitives

Reason	Example	Explanation
Clarity	"We expect profits **to approximately double** by the next fiscal year."	If "approximately" were placed after "to double" ("We expect profits to double approximately by the next fiscal year"), the result would introduce an ambiguity: it would not be clear whether it's the doubling of the profits or the time frame of the next fiscal year that's approximate. "We expect profits approximately to double" is also somewhat ambiguous because it suggests that there may be something approximate about the profits themselves (are they really profits?), rather than their doubling.

Reason	Example	Explanation
Emphasis	"**To fully satisfy** our clients, we continuously innovate."	Although the sentence could be reworded to "To satisfy our clients fully, we continuously innovate," the choice to keep "fully" next to "satisfy" emphasizes just how important full satisfaction is, and having it precede (rather than follow) "satisfy" results in natural-sounding English.
Rhythm	"We strive **to consistently outperform** our competitors."	This is a subjective judgment, but likely most readers will find the sentence to the left more rhythmic than "We strive to outperform our competitors consistently." (The wording "We strive consistently to outperform our competitors" is unadvisable because, as in the first example, it introduces an ambiguity: is it the striving or the outperforming that is consistent?)

Examples of poorly chosen split infinitives

Problem	Example	Explanation
Awkwardness	"We seek **to globally expand** our market presence."	There is no reason not to put "globally" at the end of the sentence. ("We seek to expand our market presence globally.") As with the rhythm example above, which phrasing sounds best is a matter of taste, but if there's no clear gain to be had from the split infinitive, you're better served by avoiding it.
Redundancy	"We plan **to thoroughly audit** all departments."	"Thoroughly" is implied in the context of an audit, which makes its presence in the sentence redundant.
Overemphasis	"We aim **to boldly innovate** and **disruptively change** the industry."	Multiple split infinitives can make the sentence feel overwrought and, paradoxically, can cause the sentence to lose impact.

"When I split an infinitive, god damn it, I split it so it will stay split."

— Raymond Chandler, author and screenwriter

Exercise care in the verbs you use to express assurance

Choosing the right verb to express assurance significantly influences the perceived level of commitment to an outcome. In business writing—and often in AI-generated content—"ensure" crops up with astonishing frequency, but it's a verb that makes a heavy promise. Similarly, "validate" suggests a commitment to thorough testing and assessment to verify accuracy and effectiveness. These verbs should not be selected without careful consideration. Depending on your intended message, other verbs will better align with your level of assurance and commitment.

Guidance on levels of assurance (from most to least)

Verb	Meaning	Example
Guarantee	Provides a commitment to specific results, often with a promise of recompense if the results are not achieved.	"We **guarantee** a turnaround time of no more than 24 hour for all inquiries."
Ensure	Makes sure or certain. One definition of "ensure" is "guarantee," so the level of promise is high.	"We **ensure** compliance with all regulatory standards."
Assure	Offers confidence or promises less tangible outcomes.	"We **assure** our clients of our ongoing support."
Validate	Corroborates or establishes accuracy, effectiveness or legitimacy.	"We **validate** all our products through extensive testing."
Facilitate	Makes something easier.	"We **facilitate** smoother transactions through our new platform."
Support	Assists or helps.	"We **support** our clients with 24/7 customer service."

Choose between active and passive voice to bring energy and focus

A sentence written in the active voice positions the actor before the action. In an active-voice sentence, responsibility for an action is very clear, and the actor is more important than the action. The passive voice emphasizes the object of the action or the action itself and can obscure the actor, which is appropriate when the actor's identity is irrelevant or unknown, or in certain complex or ambiguous situations.

Comparison of passive and active voice

Passive	Active	Analysis
"**The report** was prepared by the team."	"**The team** prepared the report."	Both sentences contain all the elements: the actor (the team), the object of the action (the report) and the action ("prepared"), but the first sentence emphasizes the report, while the second emphasizes the team.
"**The project** will be completed by the deadline."	"**The team** will complete the project by the deadline."	The first sentence does not include the actor: the focus is squarely on the report. The second sentence includes the actor (the team), who, as in the first example, springs forward in importance.

In most cases, use active voice

The active voice powers compelling, clear and engaging prose and should be your go-to style in most business writing. Unfortunately, the passive voice's ability to hide the actor makes it popular when people are trying to avoid blame or responsibility, which perhaps explains why passive-voice writing is so common. What follows are some suggestions for how to beat the passive-voice habit.

Guidance on successfully adopting the active voice

Strategy	Example and explanation
Identify the actor and put the actor first.	"The **manager** approved the budget." The manager is performing the action here, so put the manager first.
Avoid static "to be" verb constructions.	"The engineer **solved** the problem" is more dynamic than "The problem **was solved** by the engineer." It's also more concise.
Use strong verbs.	Instead of merely rephrasing the passive-voice sentence "First place was awarded to Team A" to "Team A won first place," consider using a more powerful verb, like "seized" or "captured." Using a dramatic verb can help remind you of the importance of foregrounding the actor. Who captured first place? Team A.

With practice, your intuitive sense of active-voice sentence construction will improve. Reading your work aloud can help you identify passive-voice sentences and other cumbersome structures.

In some situations, use the passive voice

Although generally you should try for the active voice, the passive voice has its place, particularly in formal writing or when the focus is on the object of the action or the action itself, rather than actor.

Guidance on when to use the passive voice

Circumstance	Explanation	Example
The focus is on the action or its result.	When the action is more significant than the actor or the result, passive voice downplays the actor.	"A new record **was achieved**." The focus is on the achievement rather than on who achieved it, which is unstated.
The focus is on the object of the action.	When the object of an action is more central to the message than the performer of the action, passive voice places the emphasis correctly.	"**The vaccine** was praised around the world for drastically reducing infant mortality." Here the vaccine is much more important than either the actors (unstated) or the action itself (praise).
Formality and objectivity	Although this is changing in the social sciences, formal reports and scientific literature still often use the passive voice to maintain an impersonal tone focused on the actions or findings rather than on the researchers or authors.	"The experiment **was conducted** according to protocol." This underscores the procedure, not the people conducting it.

Circumstance	Explanation	Example
Unknown or irrelevant actor	When the actor's identity is either unknown or irrelevant, the passive voice can shift focus to the action or its outcomes.	"Over 200 applications **were received**." This emphasizes the volume of applications, not the receiver.

Make sure the parts of your sentence interact harmoniously

To project assurance and mastery as a writer, you want to be sure the parts of your sentences relate to each other the way they should. If you have a singular subject, you want a singular verb—which can get complicated in some cases, but the discussion below will help. Similarly, pronouns should agree with the nouns they're replacing, and you want to be consistent in the pronouns you use.

Maintain subject-verb agreement

Knowing when to use a singular form of a verb, like "is" or "has," and when to use a plural form, like "are" or "have," is essential. While the basic rule is to use the singular form for individual entities and the plural form for multiple entities, English is filled with special cases. Let's begin with a simple example:

■ **Singular:** "The **company is** growing."

"Company" is a single entity, so use "is."

■ **Plural:** "The **companies are** competing."

Here the subject is multiple companies, so use "are."

Now let's look at some special cases.

Multiple items are sometimes treated as a single item:

■ "Research and development **is** key to innovation.

Although "research" is one item and "development" is another, "research and development," taken together, are often treated as a single item.

Some nouns are plural in form but treated as singular:

■ "The media **has** not covered that story."

"Media" is technically plural (the singular form is "medium") but it's treated as singular, hence the use of "has" rather than "have." There are other words that are plural in form but can be treated as either singular or plural depending on the field or geography you're operating in. These include the words "data," linguistics," "politics" and "statistics."

Collective nouns referring to groups of people take a singular verb in some geographies and a plural one in others:

■ The team **has** won the championship. (American English treats "team" as singular, which stresses its unity.)

■ The team **have** won the championship. (British English treats "team" as plural, which emphasizes the people making up the team.)

Following "or" or "nor," the verb aligns with the noun that's closest to it:

■ "Neither the manager nor the employees **have** backed down."

"Employees" (plural) is closer to the verb than "manager" (singular), so the verb takes the plural form, "have."

When the subject is at a distance from the verb, it's easy to make a mistake:

■ "The proposal, which covers all 10 of the major issues, **is** a work of compromise."

"Proposal," and not "issues," is the subject of the verb (it is the proposal that is a work of compromise, not the issues), even though "issues" is nearer to the verb. Therefore, the verb is singular.

Get singular and plural usage right for indefinite pronouns (e.g., "few," "most")

Indefinite pronouns, which don't refer to anything specific, can pose a challenge because they may blend into either singular or plural environments depending on the context. It is important to understand how to match them with either a singular or plural verb form.

Guidance on when to select singular or plural

Indefinite pronouns	Description and guidance	Examples (singular)	Examples (plural)
Anybody, anything, each, every, everybody, everyone, somebody, something	These indefinite pronouns all indicate single, individual nouns: any (single) body, any (single) thing, each (single), etc. "Every" may seem like the exception because it sounds inclusive, but it's used to indicate each one of the members of a group.	"Anybody **is** welcome to help." "Every piece of pizza **has** its own unique topping."	N/A
Both, few, many, plenty, several	These indefinite pronouns all indicate more than one noun and therefore take plural verbs, highlighting those collective or multiple entities.	N/A	"Both **were** silent for a moment." "Many **have** shared their thoughts on the matter."
All, most, some	When these indefinite pronouns are standing in for mass nouns—that is, nouns that indicate a homogeneous substance or concept that doesn't have subdivisions (e.g., "cement" or "freedom")—the verb form is singular. When they are standing in for countable nouns, the verb for is plural.	"Some sand **has** gotten into my shoes." "Freedom **is** a cherished right."	"Most students **have** left for the semester." "Some cookies **are** missing from the jar."
None	This indefinite pronoun can align with either singular or plural verbs, depending on the context and the emphasis on absence.	"None of the rumor **is** true." (Since the following noun, "rumor," is singular, "none" is considered singular.)	"None of the cookies **were** eaten." (Since the following noun, "cookies," is plural, "none" is treated as a plural.)

Maintain consistency in pronoun number and in person

Switching between singular and plural pronouns or inconsistently using first, second and third person can confuse readers and detract from the effectiveness of your communication. Consistency in pronouns requires that your pronoun is the same in number as your noun: if you are using a singular noun, use a singular pronoun; if you are using a plural noun, use a plural pronoun. Similarly, maintaining a consistent grammatical person ("I," "you," "we," "they") brings clarity and coherence to your narrative.

Inconsistent number example:

- **Before:** "A **team** needs to communicate effectively if **they want** to meet **their** goals."

- **After:** "A **team** needs to communicate effectively if **it wants** to meet **its** goals." (Aligns subject-verb agreement by keeping the subject and pronouns singular.)

- **Alternative:** "**Teams** need to communicate effectively if **they want** to meet **their** goals." (Adjusts the subject to plural to match with plural pronouns, maintaining consistency.)

Inconsistent person example:

- **Before:** "**We** have a long history of analyzing data. **You** look at the numbers and communicate **your** findings to **your** clients. That is why they come to **us**."

  (The sentences start out speaking in the first person plural, which is typical when speaking on behalf of an organization, but then switches to the second person, which often used in informal speech when explaining things, and then switches back to first person plural.)

- **After:** "**We** have a long history of analyzing data. **We** look at the numbers and communicate **our** findings to **our** clients. That is why they come to **us**."

  (Maintains first person plural perspective throughout the sentence.)

Use connecting and transition words properly

Connecting and transition words like "however," "but" and "because" move your narrative from one point to the next. Learn to use them effectively to enhance flow and clarify relationships between ideas in your writing.

Integrate "however" elegantly

Starting sentences with "however" is a go-to for many, but there are other ways to handle contrasts. Below are three ways to use "however" and one alternative that omits it.

- **Starting with "however":** "The initial few months were rocky. **However**, the project was ultimately a success."

- **Mid-sentence "however":** "The initial few months were rocky. The project, **however**, was ultimately a success."

- **Merge the two sentences using a semicolon:** "The initial few months were rocky; **however**, the project was ultimately a success."

- **Omitting "however":** "Although the initial months were rocky, the project ultimately succeeded."

Use "but" to bridge ideas, but get the comma right

The use of a comma before "but" depends on how it connects the parts of a sentence. A comma is generally needed when "but" precedes an independent clause, which is a group of words that can stand alone as a complete sentence. However, no comma is required when "but" links shorter, closely related ideas that do not form independent clauses. If one or both of the independent clauses are very short, you may choose not to use a comma.

- **With an independent clause:** "The company aimed to increase its market share**, but** competition was fiercer than expected."

- **Without an independent clause:** "We wanted to finalize the deal last quarter **but** encountered regulatory hurdles."

- **Two very short independent clauses with a comma:** "We sought approval**, but** it was denied."

- **The same independent clauses without a comma:** "We sought approval **but** it was denied.

Choose "because" to highlight cause and effect

Linking causes and effects accurately is vital for clarity in writing. While "as" can suggest causality, it might also imply simultaneity, leading to ambiguity. "Because" eliminates the confusion, directly establishing cause and effect.

Sometimes people use "due to" as a synonym for "because," but used correctly, "due to" has a narrower meaning: it means "attributable to" ("the mudslide was due to [attributable to] last night's heavy rains") or "owed to" ("accolades are due to [owed to] all the participants"). If you want to suggest cause and effect, use "because" in preference to "due to." Understanding the nuanced differences between "because of" and "due to" can refine your writing.

- **Before:** "Mark typed in a lot of words **as** he had nothing better to do." (Could be misunderstood to mean "Mark typed in a lot of words while he was in the state of having nothing better to do.")

- **After:** "Mark typed in a lot of words **because** he had nothing better to do." (Makes it clear that that the cause of Mark's typing in many words was that he had nothing better to do: having nothing better to do was the reason for his typing a lot of words.)

- **Before:** "The game was postponed **due to** rain."

- **After:** "The game was postponed **because of** rain." (Both convey the cause effectively, but "because of" is often clearer for directly tying actions to reasons.)

Employ "therefore" when logical connections need highlighting

"Therefore" serves as a bridge, connecting cause and effect or leading to a conclusion in an argument. Yet, when overused, it can weigh down sentences. It's essential to let the logic of your statements shine through naturally. Consider the sentence without "therefore" to see if the connection remains clear. If so, you might not need it. "Therefore" should be reserved for moments where it genuinely enhances understanding, helping to illuminate the path from premise to conclusion without acting as unnecessary padding.

Where using "therefore" can be useful:

- **Start of sentence:** "**Therefore**, we decided to increase the marketing budget." (Using "therefore" at the beginning is a formal way to introduce a conclusion based on the preceding information.)

- **Middle of sentence:** "It is with a heavy heart, **therefore**, that I announce my resignation." (Here, "therefore" is inserted as an aside, referring, as in the previous example, to preceding information that will have established the reasons for the heavy heart, such as dedication to the job or passion for the work. This use of "therefore" often adds a formal or academic tone to the sentence.)

Where "therefore" is not necessary:

- **Before:** "We failed to meet the project deadline; **therefore**, the client is dissatisfied."
- **After:** "We failed to meet the project deadline; the client is dissatisfied." (Removes "therefore" to streamline the cause-and-effect relationship.)

Go with "and" (in preference to "not only, but also") for brevity

The whole "not only, but also" setup is fancy, but rarely necessary. Sure, it adds a bit of drama and can make both parts of your statement feel equally worthy. But usually the construct sounds like it's trying a bit too hard. Stripping it down to "and" gets you to the point faster and keeps your audience's attention where it should be. Use the "not only, but also" when you're really looking to put two ideas on a pedestal, showing that they both deserve the spotlight.

- **Before:** "This writing guide is **not only** informative **but also** funny."
- **After:** "The writing guide is informative **and** funny." (Cuts out dead-weight words to deliver a straightforward, equally compelling message.)

An example of where the "not only, but also" construct is appropriate:

- "**Not only** does our company offer competitive salaries**, but** we **also** provide a comprehensive benefits package that includes health insurance, retirement plans and paid vacation."

Maintain consistency with "either/or" and "neither/nor"

In the realm of conjunctions, we often bump into this pair of dynamic duos: either/or and neither/nor. What's important to remember is that "nor" goes only with "neither," not with "either," and "or" goes only with "either," never with "neither." Basically, keep the words that start with an N together and the ones without an N together. "Either/or" is your go-to pair if you're presenting alternatives or choices where one can be true, but both cannot. "Neither/nor" is for when both alternatives are being negated (meaning neither option is applicable).

- **Before:** "**Either** the manager **nor** the employees were ready."
- **After (either/or):** "**Either** the manager **or** the employees were ready." (Corrects the misuse by pairing "either" with "or" for situations presenting alternatives.)
- **After (neither/nor):** "**Neither** the manager **nor** the employees were ready." (Correctly pairs "neither" with "nor" for negation.)

Put modifiers in the right place

Anything that describes something else is a modifier. Adjectives are the most familiar modifiers—words like "important," "strong" or "valuable." But phrases like "recently divorced" or "who was waving and smiling" can also be modifiers, and when phrases are used as modifiers, they need to be placed correctly so that they are modifying the thing you want them to modify. There are three types of misplaced modifiers—misplaced, dangling and squinting modifiers—that pose risks to clarity. The following guidance will help you identify and correct them.

Guidance on proper modifier and subject placement

Type	Explanation	Example
Misplaced modifiers	When a modifier is not right next to the thing it modifies, it can inadvertently modify something else, causing confusion. Keep modifiers close to the nouns or verbs they modify.	**Before:** "**Always available by phone, you** will find our service desk very helpful. ("Always available by phone" refers to the service desk, but as placed, it is describing "you.") **After:** "**Always available by phone**, our **service desk** is very helpful. (Now the service desk is next to the phrase that modifies it.)
Dangling modifiers	The modifier's intended subject is missing, leading to misinterpretation. The subject of the modifier should be present.	**Before:** "**Reviewing the annual report, the conclusion** was unclear." (The conclusion did not review the annual report, but who did? The subject of the modifying phrase "reviewing the annual report" is not present in the sentence.) **After:** "**Reviewing the annual report, we** found the conclusion unclear." (A subject, "we," has been introduced that makes clear who was reviewing the annual report.)
Squinting modifiers	Sometimes a modifier can be positioned such that it is not clear whether it refers to what comes before it in the sentence or what comes after it. Place modifiers such that they modify only one part of the sentence.	**Before:** "Branch offices open at 7:00 a.m. **in summer only in Iceland**." (It is unclear whether "only" refers to "in summer" or "in Iceland." In other words, it is not clear whether the sentence means that in Iceland, branch office open at 7:00 a.m. in summer only, or that only in Iceland do branch offices open at 7:00 a.m. in the summer. **After:** "In Iceland, branch offices open at 7:00 a.m. **in summer only**." **OR** "**Only in Iceland** do branch offices open at 7:00 a.m. in the summer."

Balance formality and conversational tone when using contracted words

Contractions, those shortened forms of words like "can't" for "cannot" or "it's" for "it is," can lend a conversational tone to your writing, making it more relatable. In business writing, however, contractions should be approached cautiously, with intention and awareness of context. Their informality may not always suit the professional setting or the message's gravity. The key is to strike the right balance, so your writing remains clear, professional and tailored to your audience.

Guidance on usage of contracted words

Context	Use contractions?	Example sentence
Internal communication	**Yes:** contractions are acceptable and foster a conversational tone.	"**We're** looking forward to your input."
Client correspondence	**Yes:** contractions are beneficial for creating a friendly yet professional tone.	"**We've** completed the project ahead of schedule."
Formal reports	**No:** opting for the full form emphasizes seriousness and importance.	"The company **cannot** compromise on quality."
Policy documents	**No:** avoiding contractions maintains clarity and lends a formal tone to directives.	"Employees **must not** use company resources for personal projects."

Use punctuation correctly

Punctuation basics form the bedrock of effective business communication. This section discusses some of the more troublesome punctuation marks and their proper use in business writing. Mastering these essentials will greatly improve the likelihood that your messages are understood exactly as intended.

"Punctuation is a fabulous tool for controlling your reader—you even get to control where they breathe. That's what I call power!

— Nicola Morgan, author

Use colons to lay out lists with clarity

Colons are used to introduce lists, explanations and, on occasion, quotes. They signal that what follows is directly related to what came before, and they effectively expand on or clarify that information. A colon should never interrupt a grammatically complete sentence. A good rule of thumb is that you should only use a colon if what comes before it could be a grammatically complete sentence. (For more guidance on the effective use of lists, see "Use lists to present short, related ideas or points" in Part 3.)

Example of incorrect and correct use of colons

Incorrect use	Correct use
"He **brought: wine, cheese and a guitar** to the picnic." A colon here is incorrect because "He bought" is not a grammatically complete sentence. The colon is interrupting what would otherwise be a complete and acceptable sentence ("He brought wine, cheese and a guitar to the picnic.")	"He **brought three things to the picnic: wine, cheese and a guitar**." Here the colon is used correctly. The clause that comes before it ("He brought three things to the picnic") would make a grammatically correct sentence on its own, and the list it introduces details what three things the man brought to the picnic.

Connect ideas with semicolons

Semicolons link two independent clauses that are closely related in theme but could function as standalone sentences. This punctuation mark bridges thoughts in a way that enhances the relationship between them, without the abruptness of starting a new sentence. The effect is more clipped and fast-moving than would be the case with a comma and conjunction like "and." Both clauses should, however, maintain their independence; the presence of conjunctions like "because" render the semicolon's use incorrect.

Three correct sentences with different punctuation for different effect:

- **Two independent sentences:** "After deliberation, he rejected the first proposal. He did not even consider the second."

- **Two independent clauses joined by a comma and "and":** "After deliberation, he rejected the first proposal, and he did not even consider the second."

- **Two independent clauses joined by a semicolon:** "After deliberation, he rejected the first proposal; he did not even consider the second."

Example of incorrect use of semicolon with "because"

Incorrect use	Correct use
"The company **strives to innovate; because customer satisfaction** is our top priority." The conjunction "because" introduces a dependent clause, making the semicolon inappropriate.	"The company **strives to innovate; customer satisfaction** is our top priority." This correct usage links two related but independent ideas smoothly.

Know when and how to hyphenate

Skillful use of hyphens can eliminate ambiguity, making your meaning crystal clear to the reader. Hyphenation is one of the style particulars that varies most with geography. In general, British English uses hyphens where American English will incline to eliminating hyphens and closing words up (for example, when a word has a prefix like "co" or "re" or "micro"). What follow are some commonsense guidelines.

Hyphenation can change a sentence's meaning, so use or forgo hyphens for the meaning you want:

■ "**One big bank initiative** this year is updating legacy software." (Without hyphens, the sentence is speaking about a bank initiative that is big.)

■ "**One big-bank initiative** this year is pushing for relaxation of banking regulations." (The addition of a hyphen between "big" and "bank" clarifies that here we are talking about an initiative sponsored by a big bank or banks.)

As noted above, in American English, most prefixes are joined directly to the main word without a hyphen, but sometimes a hyphen is necessary because the unhyphenated word has a different meaning.

Hyphenate words to clarify your meaning:

■ "We must **recover** the ancient books." (The ancient books have been lost; we will attempt to get them back.)

■ "We must **re-cover** the ancient books." (The covers of the ancient books are falling apart; new ones must be made.)

Hyphenate compound adjectives to improve readability:

■ "Readers struggled with the **hard to read** sentence in the report." (Although readers can probably struggle through that sentence and glean the meaning, hyphens will make it easier for them.)

■ "Readers were delighted by the improvement in the previously **hard-to-read** sentence." (Hyphens make it very clear that "hard," "to" and "read" are all part of one modifying phrase.)

Cut unnecessary words when hyphenated phrases have the same second element:

■ "Mark has **three-wheel** and **four-wheel** motorcycles." (The modifying phrases "three-wheel" and "four-wheel" share the word "wheel." That word can be eliminated.)

■ "Mark has **three- and four-wheel** motorcycles." (Note that you must leave a space after the hyphen that follows "three." It should not be joined directly to the word "and.")

Do not add a hyphen to adverbs ending in "ly":

■ Write "a **highly respected** CEO," not "a highly-respected CEO."

Add a hyphen to modifying phrase when it is before the term it modifies; do not add a hyphen if it follows that term:

■ "**State-owned** enterprises such China Power Investment Corporation were seen as having an advantage." (In front of the word "enterprises," the phrase "state-owned" has a hyphen.)

■ "Enterprises that are **state owned**, such as China Power Investment Corporation, were seen as having an advantage. (The phrase "state owned" still describes "enterprises," but because it's appearing after "enterprises," it's not hyphenated.)

Table of common words not requiring hyphenation

Antitrust	Multifaceted	Rediscover
Coordinate	Nonprofit	Reestablish
Deemphasize	Overanalyze	Suboptimal
Disenfranchise	Postoperative	Superimpose
Interconnected	Preapproval	Underestimate
Interdepartmental	Preconfigure	
Misinterpret	Recalibrate	

Use a serial (Oxford) comma with care

Nothing sparks heated grammar debates like the serial comma—the last comma before "and" in a list of items. Using a serial comma, a list of fruit would look like this: apples, pears, and mangos. Forgoing a serial comma, that list would look like this: apples, pears and mangos. The *Chicago Manual of Style* recommends using a serial comma; the *Associated Press Stylebook* recommends against it. Use of a serial comma is common in the United States; in the United Kingdom the more common rule is to use it only to avoid ambiguity. Attentive readers will note that this book does not use a serial comma, but the choice is yours. The important thing to remember is that clarity of meaning is paramount. When clarity is an issue, rephrase.

Guidance on rephrasing for clarity:

- "The event was hosted by Jennifer Garner, an actress and the cofounder of Once Upon a Farm."

  As written, without a serial comma, the statement indicates that the event was hosted by Jennifer Garner, who is an actress and cofounder of Once Upon a Farm. If that's the intended meaning, then the sentence is fine.

  If, however, the intention was to say that three people hosted, then a serial comma will help make that clear. ("The event was hosted by Jennifer Garner, an actress, and the co-founder of Once Upon a Farm.") The revised sentence still has some ambiguity, however, because readers may be unsure whether "an actress" refers to Jennifer Garner or a separate person. A better revision would supply more information to make everything clear (e.g., "The event was hosted by Jennifer Garner, actress Jessica Biel, and Once Upon a Farm cofounder John Foraker").

- "John David thanked Denzel Washington, a movie legend, and his mentor."

  Here the serial comma introduces ambiguity. It's not clear if one person, two people or three are being indicated. If one person is being indicated, the sentence could be reworded to read "John David thanked Denzel Washington, who is both a movie legend and his mentor." If two or three people are indicated, it often helps to bring in names. For two people, the sentence could be reworded to read "John David thanked Denzel Washington, who is a movie legend, and also his mentor [name]," or to "John David thanked Denzel Washington, who is his mentor, and also the movie legend [name]." If three people are indicated, the sentence could be recast to read "John David thanked three people: Denzel Washington, the movie legend [name], and his mentor [name]."

Understand how to show possession correctly with apostrophes

The most commonly practiced rule for how to form possession is that for singular subjects—and for plural subjects that don't end in "s" (e.g., children, people)—you add an apostrophe and the letter "s," and for plural subjects, you add only the apostrophe.

Singular

- "The **cat's** toy was found under the sofa."
- "The **class's** singing was heard from down the hall."
- "**James's** mother asked him to come home early."
- "**Dickens's** novels are generally fairly long."

Plural

- "The **dogs'** owner was called."
- "The **horses'** hooves sent up clouds of dust."
- "**States'** rights continue to be an issue."
- "The mission is to improve **children's** nutrition." (Plural noun that doesn't end in "s.")
- "The government was quick to smother the **people's** dissent." (Plural noun that doesn't end in "s.")

An alternative method

There are some style manuals that prefer a system where an apostrophe alone is used for all words ending in "s," whether singular or plural. (Note: this method is almost never seen in the United Kingdom.)

- "The **class'** singing was heard down the hall."
- "**James'** mother asked him to come home early."
- "**Dickens'** novels are generally fairly long."

Use advanced punctuation and styling for emphasis and engagement

The strategic use of parentheses, dashes, italics and other punctuation highlights key points and add expression to your writing. These punctuation marks, along with italicizing or bolding words, draw attention where it's needed and make your writing more forceful.

Express ranges or replace the word "to" with an en dash

There are three straight-line marks commonly used in punctuation. In order of increasing length, they are the hyphen (-), the en dash (–) and the em dash (—). Hyphens, we've already seen, are a way of joining compound words together. Often you'll also see them used for jobs that properly belong to the en dash.

En dashes are properly used for number ranges and to replace the word "to" in other contexts.

Examples of proper en dash usage

- "Please read pages **4–24** for our next meeting." (Not 4-24.)

- "The **LA–Boston** plane flies twice daily." (Not LA-Boston.)

- "The game score was **16–9**." (Not 16-9.)

In British typographic style, en dashes are used in place of em dashes (see below), but when en dashes are used in this manner, they have a space on either side of them.

Clarify and emphasize information with parentheses and em dashes

An em dash is used to indicate an abrupt interruption in the train of thought of your sentence, or, like parentheses, an inserted thought. So, when should you use em dashes and when should you use parentheses? Parentheses are your go-to for supplementary material that's informative but not critical to your main message. They subtly introduce related details without breaking the sentence's stride. In contrast, em dashes are more about effect and immediacy, perfect for creating emphasis or introducing a change of thought that's closely tied to the main sentence.

Guidance on usage of parentheses and em dashes

Punctuation	Use case	Example
Parentheses	For additional, nonessential information or to clarify or provide references without disrupting the main text.	**Clarification:** "All employees must complete the training (**mandatory as per HR guidelines**)." **Nonessential information:** "Quarterly profits rose (**see Appendix A for the full report**)."
Em dash (—)	Em dash (—)	**Emphasize pause/shift:** "Our latest product launch—**unexpectedly delayed**—is now set for Q3."
En dash (–) used as an em dash	Alternative (generally British) typographic style. Where the em dash follows directly on the word before it and is followed directly by the word after it, the en dash is used with spaces on either side of it.	"Our latest product launch – **unexpectedly delayed** – is now set for Q3."

Highlight new or important terms with italics, but avoid using them for emphasis

Use italics to call attention to new or important terms, especially in academic or technical writing. Do not use quotation marks for this purpose. (See discussion in Part 4.)

- **Term you expect may be new to the reader:** "This brings us to the concept of the *locavore*, someone who endeavors to eat only locally grown food."

- **Term or concept that is important in your text:** "*Just-in-time manufacturing*, an innovation when first introduced, is more problematic in our current era."

In speech we stress words to emphasize them, and in fiction, italics are sometimes used to capture this stress for the reader. In business writing, however, the emphasis should be implicit in the statement. The extra emotion implied by the italics is not appropriate.

- **Unadvisable:** "We will *never* share your personal information."
- **Better:** "We will never share your personal information."

Use bold text to draw attention

Bold text declares its presence assertively and is unmissable. It can be used to spotlight key directives, headlines or any element that demands attention and retention. Use bold text to highlight headings or action items to make them stand out amidst a sea of text. However, use bold sparingly so as not to dilute its effect and to avoid turning your document into a jumble of competing emphases.

- **Example:** "For our Q4 strategy, the following are the **key recommendations**:" (Bold text emphasizes the importance of the section, making it stand out for quick identification.)

Use exclamation points sparingly

Exclamation points should be reserved for occasions that genuinely warrant them, such as a sentence celebrating a significant achievement or highlighting an urgent request. Too many exclamation points will detract from the professionalism of your writing and may convey an unintended, childlike tone.

- **Inappropriate:** "Our quarterly profits rose several percentage points!" (Pleasing as this news may be, rises and declines in profit are ordinary events for businesses and therefore ordinary events in business writing. A period—or full stop, in British English—will do here.)
- **Appropriate:** "It is not every day that a former company employee is awarded the Nobel Prize for Economics!" (Demonstrates appropriate use of exclamation points to celebrate significant achievements, adding enthusiasm while maintaining professionalism.)

"What if we all took it down a notch? Made things a little less urgent? Saved exclamation points for when they really hit the spot?"

— Faith Salie, journalist, writer and actress

Use questions to provoke thought

Posing questions is a way to engage the reader and provoke thought. These questions invite consideration of the proposed viewpoint; they can emphasize a point or suggest a new perspective. You do not need to supply the answer. However, such questions should be used sparingly and purposefully so they contribute to the narrative's clarity and persuasiveness.

- **Example:** "How would employee-led performance evaluation meetings affect morale?"

Use slashes for concise options or alternatives

The slash (/) is a way to denote alternatives, dual roles or joint responsibilities. It offers shorthand for expressing options or indicating that two items are closely related or interchangeable. However, using it too frequently can clutter the text and make it difficult to read. In formal documents, consider using "or" to articulate choices more clearly when context allows, prioritizing readability.

- **Example:** "All team members are expected to participate in the **meeting/call** tomorrow." (The slash succinctly presents alternatives, offering clarity and brevity in conveying dual options or joint responsibilities.)

In this context, be precise in communicating choices. Using "and/or" muddies the waters, attempting to encompass all possibilities but often leading to confusion. Be clear: if both items are necessary, use "and"; for an either/or situation, opt for "or." When it is genuinely an open choice, "this, that or both" directly addresses all potential choices without ambiguity. Reflect on your intention—do both conditions need to be considered together or are you presenting an alternative? Your choice of conjunction should mirror your exact meaning.

- **And:** "Candidates must have experience in marketing **and** sales." (Both skills are required.)
- **Or:** "You may attend either the morning **or** afternoon session." (Only one session can be attended, not both.)
- **Both:** "Please prepare questions, statements **or both** to address to the speaker." (It clarifies that attendees can come with one, the other or both items.)

Embrace positive phrasing

We know from social media that negative messaging is good for grabbing attention, but we also know that it can be very destructive. Expressing your message in a positive way contributes to a healthier, stronger social environment, especially in a business context.

Express negatives positively for a constructive tone

One of the problems with negative prose is that often it deflates rather than energizes. A useful tactic is to employ a positive sentence structure that directs attention toward actionable outcomes rather than constraints, creating a sense of empowerment and possibility.

Effective use of positive messaging:

- **Before:** "We will **not proceed without** client approval."
- **After:** "We **will proceed once we have client approval**." (Transforms the perspective to emphasize positive action, focusing on conditions for the next step.)

Understand what double negatives convey

Double negatives are used when you want to express a hint of tacit criticism that doesn't rise to the level of full-force criticism. Consider the following sentences:

- **Positive statement:** "Employees **are satisifed** with the new policy."
- **Negative statement:** "Employees **are dissatisifed** with the new policy."

- **Double-negative statement:** "Employees **are not dissatisifed** with the new policy." (Stating that employees are not dissatisfied affirms that they are in a state that doesn't rise to the level of dissatisfaction but does not commit them to a state of satisfaction. It recognizes that there is a nuance of feeling between satisfaction and dissatisfaction.)

Always ask yourself if you really need the double negative. Would a straight-up positive or negative statement be more appropriate? Remember, too, that a double-negative statement can sound sarcastic, which is not appropriate in a business context.

Write in an inclusive and respectful style

Effective business writing demands clarity, professionalism and sensitivity. You should be selective in your choice of words and phrases, steering clear of language that could inadvertently marginalize or offend. This fosters a more inclusive and respectful business environment. Adopting an inclusive style and tone is vital for engaging a diverse audience. This section covers cultural considerations, gender-neutral language, disability awareness and avoiding violent or sexually suggestive language so your message is clear, constructive and respectful.

Adapt your style to account for cultural considerations

Effective communication with international audiences requires an awareness of cultural differences in formality, communication styles and humor. You can avoid potential misunderstandings and foster a sense of inclusivity by adjusting your writing to accommodate these differences. This means staying away of phrasing that may confuse or inadvertently offend your international readers. If you are dealing with an area or culture that's unfamiliar to you, ask for advice and pointers from colleagues from the region or those who have interacted in the region for a long time.

- **Before:** "Our expansion strategy is **to hit the ground running** in the Asian markets." (This idiom may be unfamiliar to nonnative English speakers, who may be confused if they take "hit the ground" literally.)

- **After:** "Our expansion strategy is **to quickly establish our presence** in the Asian markets **through strategic partnerships and local marketing**." (In addition to adding concrete details, this wording avoids the idiom and is more respectful.)

- **Before:** "To successfully enter the European market, we'll **employ a guerrilla marketing strategy** that aggressively targets consumers." (The war metaphor can be painful in geographies that are threatened by or have experienced conflict.)

- **After:** "To enter the European market, we plan to **adopt an innovative marketing strategy**, carefully tailored to respect and engage with local customs and consumer preferences." (This alternative adds more detail and highlights the importance of adapting marketing strategies to fit cultural contexts, fostering respect and inclusivity.)

Use gender-neutral language

In today's diverse and inclusive business environment, you should adopt gender-neutral language. Simple steps, such as shifting from the exclusive use of "he" or the clumsy "he/she" to the inclusive "they" and opting for ungendered job titles and descriptions, will make your writing respectful and professional.

Pronoun use example:

- **Before:** "When a client asks for a meeting, **he or she** should be given a prompt response."
- **After:** "When a client asks for a meeting, **they** should be given a prompt response." (Uses "they" as a singular, gender-neutral pronoun.)

  Note: Although the singular "they" has been used for centuries, you still may receive pushback if you use it. If you do, see if you can reword to a plural subject: "When **clients** ask for a meeting, **they** should be given a prompt response."

Job title example:

- **Before:** "The **chairman** will address the board."
- **After:** "The **chair** will address the board." (Updates job title to be gender neutral.)

Describing roles example:

- **Before:** "The **female engineer** will present the report."
- **After:** "The **engineer** will present the report." (Focuses on the role rather than gender; the addition of "female" is only needed if it's directly relevant to the discussion.)

Avoid language that discriminates in favor of able-bodied people

Language that overlooks the experiences of individuals with disabilities can inadvertently propagate attitudes that discriminate in favor of able-bodied people (ableism). Such expressions, though often used without bad intent, can reinforce negative stereotypes or and inadvertently promote exclusion. By choosing words carefully, you can express your thoughts in a respectful manner that is welcoming to all readers. This includes opting for people-first language, which emphasizes the person, not the disability (e.g., "colleagues with dyslexia" rather than "dyslexic colleagues" or "dyslexics").

Examples of discriminatory language

Inappropriate phrase	Revised phrase
"We've identified a **blind spot** in our strategy."	"We've identified an **overlooked area** in our strategy."
"Our leadership is **schizophrenic**, hopping from one strategy to another."	"Our leadership **lacks consistency, oscillating between** strategies."
"The new department is finally **standing on its own two feet**."	"The new department is now **becoming independent and self-sufficient**."
"Our team is **tone-deaf** in its messaging."	"Our team is **insensitive** in its messaging."

Avoid violent or sexually suggestive language

In business communication, it's crucial to stay away from violent language and the language of sexual innuendo. Expressions that were historically commonplace can now alienate or disturb your audience. By opting for language that clearly conveys your intentions without resorting to such expressions, you maintain the integrity and inclusivity of your message.

Examples of violent phrases

Inappropriate phrase	Revised phrase
"Let's **kill two birds** with one stone."	"Let's efficiently **achieve multiple goals**."
"Let's not **throw the baby out** with the bathwater."	"**Let's preserve** valuable elements **while making changes.**"
"We must **weaponize** our offerings."	"We must **enhance the competitiveness** of our offerings."

Examples of sexually suggestive phrases

Inappropriate phrase	Revised phrase
"We need to **get into bed** with the competition."	"We should **consider strategic partnerships** with our competitors."
"The board is getting **into management's shorts**."	"The board is **getting too involved in management's** day-to-day operations."

Use direct, accessible language

Simplicity can transform your writing from good to great. This section champions the use of accessible language, the avoidance of clichés and jargon and the importance of succinctness.

Replace clichés and colloquialisms with common prose

While often-repeated phrases may initially appear appealing, they can come across as clichéd and worn. Colloquialisms, being inherently local in nature, are prone to misinterpretation and can cause confusion. It's advisable to avoid both as much as possible.

Examples of overused clichés and simpler alternatives

Phrase	Meaning	Alternative
At the end of the day	Signifies what's really important	In conclusion Ultimately
Back to the drawing board	Implies starting over	Begin anew Start over
Break the ice	Refers to initiating a conversation	Introduce ourselves Start the conversation

Phrase	Meaning	Alternative
Burn the midnight oil	Work late into the night	Extend our hours Work late
Circle back	Intended to revisit a topic later	Follow up on this topic Revisit this discussion
Don't put all your eggs in one basket	Warns against overcommitment to one option	Avoid putting all resources into one area Don't rely on a single option
Don't reinvent the wheel	Warns against unnecessary re-creation of existing solutions	Build on what we already know Use existing methods
Drank the Kool-Aid	Uncritically accepted something (Original meaning: uncritically accepted something dangerous or problematic)	Rashly embraced Uncritically accepted
It's a win-win	Describes a situation where all parties benefit	All sides benefit Mutually beneficial
Low-hanging fruit	Tasks or goals that are easily achievable	Easy targets Quick wins
Move the needle	Making significant progress	Achieve significant progress Have a measurable effect
On the same page	In agreement	In agreement Aligned on this
Peel the onion	Examine layers of a complex problem	Analyze in depth Examine layer by layer
Push the envelope	Go beyond conventional limits	Explore new boundaries Go beyond limits
Put a pin in that one	Pause or delay discussion	Let's revisit this later We'll table this topic for future discussion
Take it offline	Suggests discussing the matter privately, not in the current forum or meeting	Convene after Discuss privately
Take it to the next level	Indicates elevating a project, idea or relationship to a higher standard or stage	Enhance Elevate
Think outside the box	Calls for creativity	Explore unconventional ideas Think creatively
Tip of the iceberg	Indicates there's more to something than is initially evident	A hint at a larger issue Just the beginning

Use plain English instead of foreign-origin terms

While using foreign-origin terms can add a touch of sophistication, it may alienate readers unfamiliar with the language. Always be clear and inclusive in business communications by using plain-English alternatives.

Examples of overused foreign-origin terms and simpler alternatives

Term	Definition	Alternative
Ad hoc	Something formed or used for a specific purpose	Purpose-built Specifically designed
Bona fide	Used to describe something genuine or real	Authentic Genuine
Caveat emptor	Buyer beware	Be wary as a buyer Buyer's caution
De facto	Practices that exist in reality even if not officially recognized	Actual In practice
Ex ante/ex post	Assessments before and after an event	After the fact Beforehand In retrospect
Lingua franca	A common language used among people with diverse home languages	Common language
Per se	Indicates something in itself or intrinsically	By itself Inherently
Quid pro quo	A favor or advantage granted in return for something	Mutual exchange Reciprocal arrangement
Status quo	Maintaining current conditions	Current state Existing conditions
Vis-à-vis	In relation to or compared with	Compared to In relation to

Opt for straightforward words instead of corporate jargon

Corporate jargon might have its place in meetings (a point open to debate), but it tends to undermine the quality of your writing. Choosing simple words over complex jargon enhances clarity with no sacrifice of sophistication.

Examples of corporate jargon and simpler alternatives

Jargon	Alternative	Edited example
Actionable	Practical	"These insights are ~~actionable~~ **practical** for our strategy."
Commencement	Beginning or start	"The ~~commencement~~ **start** of the project is scheduled for next week."
Connectivity	Connection	"This tool improves the ~~connectivity~~ **connection** between teams."
Facilitation	Assistance or help	"Her ~~facilitation~~ **help** with the project was invaluable."
Functionality	Usefulness, capability, ability	"The new software update enhances its **usefulness for** data analysis ~~functionality~~."
Ideate	Brainstorm or imagine	"Let's work as a team to ~~ideate~~ **brainstorm** new possibilities."
Level-setting	Establishing a baseline	"We need a meeting ~~for level-setting~~ **to establish a baseline**."
Methodology	Method	"The project's success depends on the chosen ~~methodology~~ **method**."
Mission-critical	Essential	"This ~~mission-critical~~ **essential** task"
Negative growth	Decline	"The company experienced ~~negative growth~~ **a decline**."
Operationalization	Putting something into use or making it useable	"The ~~operationalization~~ of new technologies can be challenging." → "**Putting** new technologies **into use** can be challenging."
Rounding error	Insignificant issue or minor matter	"We can ignore that; it's just a ~~rounding error~~ **minor matter**."
Specifications	Details	"The ~~specifications~~ **details** of the agreement were carefully reviewed."
Synergy	Cooperation	"We aim to achieve ~~synergy~~ **cooperation** between our departments for better outcomes."
Termination	End	"The contract's ~~termination~~ **end** is effective immediately."
Touch point	Contact or interaction	"Our next ~~touch point~~ **contact** with the client."

Communicate maturity with appropriate (e.g., "best," "leading") practice levels

In business writing, it's important to understand various levels of practice adoption to accurately convey the maturity or novelty of methods within an industry. You should choose terms like "best" or "leading" only to describe practices that truly are best or leading. Use of those adjectives to describe practices that would more accurately be described as "common" or "widespread" can undermine the credibility of your writing and diminish the reader's respect for your perspective. Your writing should reflect the current state of industry practices so that readers can make informed decisions based on a realistic understanding of the field.

Guidance on three levels of industry adoption of practices

Phrase	Meaning	Example (technology)
Common practice	Tried-and-true methods universally recognized for their reliability	"Using cloud storage for data backup is a common practice among businesses."
Best practice	Gold-standard methods backed by evidence and industry approval	"Implementing multifactor authentication (MFA) for system access is considered a best practice for enhancing security."
Leading practice	Cutting-edge methods that are setting new standards because they show tangible benefits beyond the theoretical	"Adopting blockchain technology for secure and transparent transactions is a leading practice in financial services."

Forgo sporting metaphors

While popular, sporting metaphors can alienate readers who are unfamiliar with the sports referenced. Replace them with more widely understood language.

Examples of overused sporting metaphors and simpler alternatives

Phrase	Meaning and origin	Alternative
Ballpark figure	A rough estimate, with origins in baseball stadiums	Approximate number Rough estimate
Call an audible	Suggesting a sudden strategic shift, from football terminology	Adjust our strategy Alter our approach
Drop the ball	Suggests a mistake or oversight, borrowing from various sports	Missed a detail Overlooked an element
Huddle up	From football, where players gather to set their play strategy, used in business contexts to mean to meet or discuss	Gather for a discussion Time for a meeting

Phrase	Meaning and origin	Alternative
Keep your eye on the ball	Reminder to maintain focus, from baseball	Keep attention on the goal Stay focused on the objective
Knock it out of the park	Aiming to impress or excel, from baseball	Achieve great success Excel in reaching our goals
Off the back foot	Indicates a defensive stance or disadvantage, from cricket	Facing challenges In a reactive position
Overclubbing it	Indicating excessive force or complexity, from golf	Let's simplify our approach We're overcomplicating things
Step up to the plate	Calls for taking responsibility or initiative, from baseball	Lead this effort Take responsibility

Avoid turning nouns into verbs

Transforming nouns into verbs can obscure your writing. Opt for simple verbs to uphold grammatical integrity and maintain the action-oriented nature of your prose.

Examples of nouns used as verbs and alternatives

Noun used as a verb	Alternative	Edited example
Action	Complete	"We need to ~~action~~ complete these tasks."
Architect	Design	"The team will ~~architect~~ design a proposal."
Dialogue	Talk	"Let's ~~dialogue~~ talk further tomorrow."
Leverage	Use	"How will you ~~leverage~~ use your unique skills?"
Solution	Solve	"You need to ~~solution~~ solve this issue."
Task	Assign	"Caden was ~~tasked with~~ assigned to train the temp worker."
Ticket	Log or record	"Have you ~~ticketed~~ logged this event?"
Workshop	Develop	"Soren needs to ~~workshop~~ develop that idea further."

Avoid selecting the wrong word from commonly confused pairs

With hundreds of thousands of words in the English language, it's understandable that professionals often make mistakes in word choice. In some cases, an incorrect word may not significantly alter the intended meaning. In others, the effect can be substantial. At times, the confusion stems merely from the differences between American and British English.

> "You keep using that word. I do not think it means what you think it means."
>
> — Inigo Montoya in *The Princess Bride* (1987)

To excel as a writer, you can't simply assume you've chosen the right word. You must intentionally choose the word that best expresses your intended meaning, and if you have even the slightest suspicion that it's a word that's often confused with another word, or if you have sometimes seen it used in ways that give you pause, check a dictionary. The table below highlights pairs of words that writers frequently confuse. Appendix 2 includes other words that are often mixed up or used erroneously.

Examples of commonly confused terms

Words	Contrasting usage	Explanation Note: with word definitions, only the relevant definitions are given.
Accept or except	"We ~~except~~ accept all major credit cards." "We host websites in all countries ~~accept~~ except North Korea, South Sudan and the Central African Republic."	"Accept" means to receive willingly; "except" signals an exclusion.
Advice or advise	"Aurora always has very good ~~advise~~ advice in situations like this." "Please ~~advice~~ advise us on the next steps."	"Advice" is a noun: it's the thing that's given, received and sought after in difficult situations. It can mean "counsel" (noun form) or "recommendations." "Advise" is the verb form; it's the action of giving counsel or making a recommendation.
Affect or effect	"The new policy will ~~effect~~ affect our project timelines." [The new policy will do something that causes a change] "The ~~affects~~ effects of the new policy were significant and widespread." [The consequences of new policy were significant.]	These two words are among the most frequently confused, in part because they have (less common) meanings that undercut their more common meanings. Checking a dictionary when you want to use one of these words is your best protection, but a quick rule of thumb for most cases is that "affect" is usually a verb that means "to do something that causes a change in something else," whereas "effect" is usually a noun that means "result, outcome, consequence."

Words	Contrasting usage	Explanation
		Note: with word definitions, only the relevant definitions are given.
Bring or take	"Kathryn, please ~~bring~~ take the documents to the downtown office [which is not where I am]." "Kathryn, please ~~take~~ bring the documents to the downtown office [where I am waiting for them]."	"Bring" implies movement toward the speaker, while "take" is correct for moving items away from the speaker. If you are moving items or requesting that items be moved away from you, use "take," but if you are moving items or requesting that items be moved to you, use "bring."
Complement or compliment	"Your skills ~~compliment~~ complement those of the rest of the team perfectly." "She ~~complemented~~ complimented the team on bringing the project to completion early."	"Compliment" means to praise; "complement" means to complete or go well with.
Compose or comprise	"Many experts ~~comprise~~ compose the team." "Our team ~~composes~~ comprises many experts. "Our team is composed of many experts."	"Comprise" means "to include," while "compose" means "to make up." Although "is comprised of" is becoming more common, some style manuals consider it improper. If you find yourself wanting to use a passive construction, using "is composed of" will keep the style quibblers at bay.
Continual or continuous	"Our network experiences ~~continuous~~ continual updates." "The Centennial Light holds the record for the light bulb with the longest ~~continual~~ continuous operation."	"Continuous" means without interruption, whereas "continual" means ongoing, but with breaks.
Farther or further	"New York is ~~further~~ farther away from London than Paris is." "We need to look ~~farther~~ further into this issue."	"Farther" refers to physical distance; "further" is used for abstract extension or advancement.
Imply or infer	"Based on the data, we can ~~imply~~ infer the company went through a turbulent patch in the last decade." "He presented graphs showing a sharp upward trend in profits after the change in CEO, strongly ~~inferring~~ implying that that a new vision at the helm was responsible for the turnaround."	"Imply" is what the speaker, writer or evidence does (suggests, hints); "infer" is what the listener or reader does (deduces, draws a conclusion).
Principal or principle	"We will never violate the ~~principal~~ principle of transparency." "The ~~principle~~ principal reason for her success is her hard work."	"Principal" can be a noun meaning a person of high authority or an adjective meaning main or most important. "Principle" can only be a noun. It means a fundamental law, doctrine or rule.

Avoid hyperbole when emphasis is required

It's tempting to grab attention by using powerful adjectives, but it's important to be thoughtful in their use. Using adjectives like "agile" or "cutting-edge" when all you really mean is "good" merely dilutes the power of those words and may ring false if, in fact, the process, program or feature you are describing is not agile or cutting-edge. Remember too, there's a fine line between emphasis and overstatement.

Examples of commonly used adjectives that can be hyperbolic

Adjective	The problem	Recommendation
Agile	Misuse dilutes its specific meaning (nimble, dexterous) in methodologies.	Use specifically for systems/methodologies emphasizing adaptability.
Best-ever	Creates unrealistic expectations; sounds boastful.	Use very sparingly, preferably only in ad copy or promotional material.
Comprehensive	Claims often fall short of covering everything, which is what "comprehensive" promises.	Use when you can substantiate all-encompassing coverage.
Cutting-edge	Overused, lessening its effect.	Reserve for advancements that truly are at the forefront in the field.
Dynamic	Can be ambiguous without clarification.	Clarify what makes the subject dynamic.
Fail-proof	Suggests infallibility, which is nearly impossible.	Use "reliable," which conveys robustness without overpromising.
Game-changing	Overuse leads to skepticism.	Reserve for innovations that fundamentally alter practices.
Holistic	Often overpromises what is included.	Specify how the subject is holistic.
Impactful	Lacks precision and is overused.	Specify the type of effect, or use "significant" or "influential."
Insightful	Overused for common findings.	Reserve for observations or analyses that demonstrate profound understanding.
Interesting	Used as a polite acknowledgment, can be seen as damning with faint praise.	Reserve for genuinely intriguing or novel content and follow up with information that demonstrates why the content is interesting.
Revolutionary	Inappropriately used to describe minor changes.	Use only for innovations that drastically change the current state.
Seamless	Rarely achieved; often overpromises.	Use when integrations or experiences truly have no discernible flaws or interruptions.
Synergistic	Claims of enhanced outcomes due to multiple cooperative inputs are often exaggerated.	Provide concrete examples to justify its use.

Adjective	The problem	Recommendation
Unique	Inappropriately used to describe things that are slightly unusual, not truly one-of-a-kind.	Use for features or offerings that are genuinely one-of-a-kind.
Unprecedented	Few situations are truly without precedent.	Use only for situations that truly warrant it.
World-class	Ambiguous and subjective without defined standards.	Define specific standards met to give it meaning.

Avoid overuse of "ize" verbiage

The number of verbs ending in "ize" that get drafted into use in business writing is astonishing. In almost every case, there's a simpler, more accessible alternative.

Examples of "ize" words and simpler alternatives

Verb	Alternative	Edited example
Actualize	Achieve	"We aim to ~~actualize~~ **achieve** our goals in the next quarter."
Calendarize	Schedule	"We need to ~~calendarize~~ **schedule** the next meeting."
Customize	Adjust	"~~Customize~~ **Adjust** the settings to fit your needs."
Finalize	Complete	"Please ~~finalize~~ **complete** the document by Friday."
Globalize	Expand internationally	"We need to ~~globalize~~ **expand** our operations **internationally**."
Incentivize	Motivate	"We need to ~~incentivize~~ **motivate** our employees with rewards."
Itemize	List	"Please ~~itemize~~ **list** all the expenses for the project."
Monetize	Earn from	"The company plans to ~~monetize~~ **earn from** each unique page view."
Optimize	Improve	"~~Optimize~~ **Improve** the process to increase efficiency."
Prioritize	Rank or order	"We need to ~~prioritize~~ **rank** our project milestones."
	Address or handle first	"We need to ~~prioritize~~ **handle** the NewData account first.
Synthesize	Combine or produce [through combining disparate elements]	"We need to ~~synthesize~~ **combine** the data." **OR** "We need to ~~synthesize~~ **produce** a new approach."
Utilize	Use	"Please ~~utilize~~ **use** the standard template for the report."

Be succinct

Being succinct requires the courage not to hide behind a hedge of protective qualifying statements. It takes bravery to make a statement without leaving room for retreat—to say, "Meetings last between one and two hours" rather than couching that with a "Generally" or "In most cases." But those words and phrases are weak protection and add unnecessary verbiage. Instead, find the statements you can make without equivocation.

> "Don't use seven words when four will do."
>
> — Rusty Ryan in *Ocean's Eleven* (2001)

Avoid weakening superlatives

Some words represent concepts at the extreme ends of a spectrum. They are superlatives—words like "best," "perfect" or "unanimous," for example. Undercutting such words by adding qualifiers such as "almost" or "nearly" muddles their clear-cut meaning, creating paradoxical statements that diminish the strength and clarity of your message. If you don't have the confidence to use the unadorned superlative, pick a different word.

Examples of qualified superlatives and simpler alternatives

Superlative with example modifier	Aims to communicate	Alternative sentence
Absolute: "almost absolute"	Specify the degree of certainty or authority	"The supervisory board **has final authority over all decisions, except** the appointment of the auditor."
Complete: "nearly complete"	Status update	"The project is in its final phase, **95% complete**."
Empty: "nearly empty"	Quantify what's left	"The container is at **10% capacity**."
Identical: "nearly identical"	Highlight exact similarities	"The two models share the **same specifications**."
Inevitable: "almost inevitable"	Express certainty about future outcomes	"Given the market trends, this outcome is **highly likely**."
Perfect: "practically perfect"	Highlight the specific achievements	"The **timing and rollout** of the strategy were **perfect**."
Total: "almost total"	Emphasize breadth of coverage	"The new policy covers **all situations except** natural disasters, warfare and epidemic disease."
Unanimous: "virtually unanimous"	Indicate the level of agreement	"**Eleven of the 12** board members supported the proposal."
Unique: "very unique"	Specify the singular quality	"The AI-driven solution **is unique in being self-improving**."
Universal: "almost universal"	Discuss the extent of acceptance	"The policy enjoys **broad support** across the organization."

Eliminate superfluous modifiers (e.g., "generally")

Bland modifiers serve only to clutter your writing and weaken the effect of your message. Whenever feasible, avoid them altogether.

Examples of unnecessary modifiers

Modifier	Reasons for avoiding use	Edited example
Actually	Can imply surprise or be used for corrections or clarifications, but it is unnecessary.	"The news reported him in a dead heat with Kirui, but Cherono ~~actually~~ won the race."
Basically	Suggests oversimplification.	"We are ~~basically~~ over budget."
Currently	Often superfluous as the immediacy is implied.	"We are ~~currently~~ experiencing delays."
Definitely	Implies certainty that might not be necessary.	"We ~~definitely~~ need to reconsider."
Eventually	Implies an uncertain timeline.	"We will ~~eventually~~ find a solution."
Finally	Suggests a long wait or struggle, might be exaggerated.	"We ~~finally~~ reached a conclusion."
Generally	Weakens the statement.	"It's ~~generally~~ considered unsafe."
Honestly	Unnecessary; implies other statements might be dishonest.	"~~Honestly~~ Option three is best."
Just	Is unnecessarily concessive.	"I ~~just~~ think it's wrong."
Literally	An unnecessary intensifier for statements.	"The team ~~literally~~ worked all night."
Maybe	Introduces uncertainty.	"We can ~~maybe~~ try a different approach."
Perhaps	Equivocates; suggests timidity in making the statement.	"We ~~perhaps~~ should start over."
Quite	Has different shades of meaning in different parts of the English-speaking world; avoid.	"The results are ~~quite~~ significant."
Really	Adds little value; often redundant.	"This is ~~really~~ important."
Somewhat	Vague; weakens effect of the statement.	"It's ~~somewhat~~ difficult."
Very	Overused for emphasis; can be eliminated for stronger effect.	"She was ~~very~~ happy."

The word "literally" deserves a special mention, beyond its frequent overuse as an intensifier. Over the years, "literally" has been used to mean "'in effect'" or "virtually," especially before a statement or metaphor that is clearly not true or possible. For example, "The team was literally on fire at the competition" suggests an impossibility. To those particular about language (including this author), the correct clarifier for such a metaphor is "figuratively," not "literally" (albeit no one would actually say "the team was figuratively on fire"). The simplest way to avoid irritating your readers is to refrain from using literally.

A man is not very tired, he's exhausted. And don't use very sad, use … morose."

— John Keating in *Dead Poets Society* (1989)

Avoid preambles and uninformative qualifying statements when stating your opinion

Beating about the bush and adding too many qualifying statements can obscure your message and diminish the strength of your argument. Instead, streamline your writing so your audience receives your message exactly as you intend. Make your statements more direct and influential.

Guidance on cutting preambles and unnecessary qualifying statements

Phrase	Guidance
Albeit not without exception	Simplify to "Although there are exceptions."
By and large	Just state your point.
For all intents and purposes	Just state your point.
Given the fact that	Use "because" or "since" for brevity.
In a manner of speaking	Just state your point.
It goes without saying	Just state your point.
It is worth mentioning that	Just state your point.
Notwithstanding the fact that	Simplify to "despite" or "although."

Only use "agreed upon" and "approved" when needed

Business writers sometimes try to boost the legitimacy of their message with qualifiers like "agreed upon" or "approved," but these adjectives are rarely necessary. The term "agreed upon" is best reserved for when it's crucial to emphasize consensus among all parties involved, such as in legal agreements or collaborative projects. It highlights that a mutual decision has been reached. Conversely, "approved" should be employed when it's necessary to indicate that an authoritative figure or body has formally sanctioned something. "Approved" signals that an official endorsement has been given, an authorization rather than collective agreement.

- **Agreed upon:** "All units of the company were involved in suggesting, creating and revising the strategies. Five months later, the **agreed-upon** strategies were implemented." (Emphasizes consensus among parties before action, highlighting the collective-agreement aspect. Note that "agreed upon" has a hyphen in the example sentence because it comes directly before "strategies," the word it's modifying.)

- **Approved:** "In a press release, the regulator announced which policies it had approved and which it had rejected. The **approved** policies will take effect next month." (Indicates formal endorsement or sanction by an authority rather than collective agreement.)

Eliminate "the fact that"

"The fact that" is a common phrase that often serves only to lengthen sentences without adding value. Its usage can create a barrier between the reader and the main point you're trying to make. In most cases, you can omit "the fact that" entirely without losing any meaning, making your writing sharper and more forceful.

- **Before:** "**The fact that** the team worked overtime did not go unnoticed."
- **After:** "The team's overtime work did not go unnoticed."

Use time-related qualifiers only when needed

When discussing timelines, future plans or the timeliness of your writing, qualifiers related to time add distinct nuances. You should select the most fitting temporal expression to accurately convey your intended meaning.

Guidance on temporal phrases and when to use them

Phrase	Meaning	Example
As of	Specifies timeliness of information.	"**As of** this report, profits total $1 million."
As yet	Indicates something hasn't happened but might in the future.	"**As yet**, we have not decided on the final design."
Going forward	Denotes future actions or strategies from this point on.	"**Going forward**, we'll adopt a more agile development process."
In the foreseeable future	Used for expected outcomes without a specific timeframe.	"We plan to expand our operations in **the foreseeable future.**"
To date	Summarizes events or outcomes up until the current point.	"**To date**, the software upgrade has reduced processing times by 30%."

* * * * *

Embracing simplicity in your writing paves the way for clear and effective communication. By avoiding jargon, being succinct and choosing straightforward words, you make your business writing accessible to all. Next, we will explore how to effectively use visuals and data to complement your clear and precise writing.

PART

Data
Presentation

Good business writing always involves the creation of a narrative to convey information, and very often that information involves data. This section guides you both in using data effectively in your written narrative and in selecting appropriate visuals (e.g., graphs and tables) to support and amplify your message. You will learn how to make data relatable, maintain its integrity and creatively present information (e.g., by using subheadings and lists).

In Part 3

- Focus on audience comprehension.
- Use visuals for enhanced communication.
- Use structural tools to enhance readability.
- Structure data effectively in tables.
- Elevate your stories with charts.

Focus on audience comprehension

Your audience needs to understand the story you're telling with your data, which means you must present your data in a way that is accessible and captivating, irrespective of the audience's familiarity with data analysis. Innovative data visualization lets you capitalize on the picture-is-worth-a-thousand-words phenomenon, allowing you to speak to your audience in a whole new language.

Guidance on audience comprehension

Strategy	Guidance
Consider your audience's knowledge level	Complex data presentations and specialized language is appropriate for experts, but simplify your presentation for a general audience. You will present financial data differently to accountants than to a general business audience, for example.
Adapt tone	Choose a professional and formal tone in discussing data for academic or business audiences and a conversational tone for a broader public audience.
Contextualize data and provide examples	**Context:** Explain the relevance of the data to your audience, whether that audience is an industry, a company or the interested public. **Examples:** Employ analogies and metaphors to make complex data understandable, using examples familiar to your audience.

Explore creative approaches to using data

Deploying data in a way that strikes a chord with the audience requires a blend of empathy, creativity and storytelling finesse. Each strategy outlined below will help you unearth the narrative within the numbers, enabling you to craft stories that inform, resonate and leave a lasting impression.

"Data is like garbage. You'd better know what you are going to do with it before you collect it."

— Attributed to Mark Twain, writer

Guidance on bringing creativity to using data

Strategy	Description
Ask questions	Start by exploring the data's implications: who it affects, the story it tells and its significance. This approach can uncover the human element or broader context, which will help in crafting relatable narratives.
Brainstorm with others	Collaborate for fresh perspectives. Discussion can lead to new connections and narratives previously overlooked.
Embrace metaphors and analogies	Connect data to everyday experiences or familiar phenomena, making large numbers or complex concepts more tangible and understandable.
Focus on the effect	Assess how the data affects individuals, communities or the environment, highlighting its real-world implications and emotional resonance.
Look for the unexpected	Identify surprising patterns, anomalies or trends. Unexpected findings can challenge expectations and form intriguing stories.
Reverse your perspective	View the data from the standpoint of different stakeholders (customers, employees, competitors) to uncover unique angles and insights.
Simplify complex concepts	Break down intricate data or ideas into simpler pieces, focusing on those core components to uncover narrative approaches.
Use visual aids	Employ graphs and charts to visualize data. Visual representations can highlight trends and insights that numbers alone might not reveal.

Guidance on data storytelling: Illustrative examples

The essence of data storytelling is more than visualization; it involves connecting data to the human experience, making abstract numbers feel personal and persuasive.

Strategy	Description	Initial example	Revised example
Emphasize effect	Focus on how the data affects the reader or the subject matter directly, making the stakes clear.	"Energy consumption has been reduced by 25%."	"Your lights are just as bright, and your world just as warm, but now with a quarter less strain on our planet. It's a step toward sustainability that illuminates a brighter future for us all."
Emphasize the human element	Connect the data to the people behind it or those affected by it.	"Employee training programs have expanded by 40%."	"Behind every number is a story, and in this case, it's the tale of our dedicated employees embarking on a 40% richer learning journey, paving their path to mastery and fulfillment."
Highlight contrasts and comparisons	Use contrasts to starkly showcase differences, making the data's implications more vivid.	"32% of our leadership team are women."	"While nearly a third of the seats at our leadership table are occupied by women, that number starkly contrasts with the remaining two-thirds. It's a gap we're committed to closing."

Strategy	Description	Initial example	Revised example
Incorporate storytelling elements	Use setting, characters and plot to frame your data within a story to engage readers.	"Our software increases assembly line efficiency by 40%."	"We were desperate to increase our output, but new infrastructure outlays were out of the question. Then our technology partners came to the rescue with a software fix that got us an extra three hours' worth of production each shift. We were saved."
Incorporate visual language	Use descriptive, vivid language that helps the reader "see" the data.	"Last year our nonprofit preserved 91,000 acres of farmland."	"The continued existence of those fields of gold-tasseled corn and those blueberry patches your kids love to visit is made possible thanks to our work keeping farmland under cultivation—to date, acreage equal to twice the size of Cape Cod."
Personify data	When possible, bring data to life by associating it with human characteristics or actions.	"This quarter, customer satisfaction increased by 20%."	"This quarter, our customers have voiced their approval louder than ever before, with a wave of satisfaction that's surged by a fifth compared to our last measure."
Use familiar comparisons	Relate data to well-known sizes, places or experiences to give your audience a frame of reference.	"The new warehouse covers 50,000 square meters."	"Almost 10 American football fields in size, our new warehouse is a testament to our expansive growth."
Use historical comparisons	Compare your data to historical events or trends to show progress or significance.	"We have doubled our research and development budget since 2020."	"Just as President Kennedy was committed to spending what it took to put a man on the moon, our board and c-suite are fully committed to funding our current research initiatives. This is our moon shot, and the doubling of our research and development budget since 2020 puts success within our reach."
Use metaphors	Employ metaphors to convey the essence of the data in a more relatable or striking manner.	"Our customer base has grown by 30% this year."	"Under the attentive care of our new marketing director, who has nurtured long-standing relationships and planted new ones, our customer base hasn't just expanded; it has burgeoned, growing 30% this year. Now that's a green thumb!"

Contextualize your data

Simplifying statistics and employing contextual conversions are strategies that demystify complex data, making it approachable and understandable.

Examples of simplifying or contextualizing data

Type	Original	Simplified	Description
Intuitive simplification	15%	Roughly 1 in 7	Transforms a percentage into a more tangible fraction for ease of understanding.
	64%	About 2 in 3	Rounds a percentage to a familiar fraction, making the proportion easier to visualize.
	0.2%	1 in 500	Converts a small percentage into a fraction, highlighting rarity or likelihood.
Contextual conversions	2.5 million square kilometers	About the size of Argentina	Provides a geographical comparison to convey the vastness of an area.
	21 petabytes of data	Equivalent to Library of Congress's digital collection in 2021	Illustrates the enormity of data by comparing it to a large, known library.
	150 liters of water	Enough to fill a small bathtub	Offers a daily life comparison to visualize volume.
	900 kilowatt-hours	Enough energy to power an average US home for a month	Translates energy production or consumption into a relatable household figure.
	4 million visitors	More than the population of Los Angeles	Compares event attendance to the size of a well-known city, highlighting scale.
	10 tons	Equivalent to about 5 cars	Translates a measure of weight into a quantity of familiar objects, clarifying scale.
	A trillion dollars	Roughly the GDP of the Netherlands	Relates a financial figure to the economic output of a country, emphasizing its magnitude.

In contexts such as finance or financial risk management, you may want to convey the potential error rate of data through statistical confidence intervals. Common confidence levels are 95%, 99.5% and 99.9%. If your reader isn't familiar with these levels, it's helpful to explain them in simpler terms. While 95% is obviously lower, 99.5% and 99.9% may seem similar at first glance. However, these levels of confidence are very different, as a reader can understand when they are explained.

Confidence level	Number that might fall outside expected range
95%	1 in 20
99.5%	1 in 200
99.9%	1 in 1,000

By explaining the percentages in this way, you can give your reader a better understanding of the differences and implications of each confidence level.

Uphold integrity when presenting data

When presenting data in business writing, maintaining accuracy and integrity is paramount. This commitment means the data shared is trustworthy and that its presentation is honest, transparent and respects the intelligence of the audience. Misrepresenting data, whether intentionally or by oversight, can significantly damage your credibility and the trust readers place in your analysis.

> "There are two ways of lying. One, not telling the truth and the other, making up statistics."
>
> — Josefina Vazquez Mota, economist and politician

All data presented should be correct, up-to-date and sourced from reliable research or databases. Inaccuracies can lead to incorrect conclusions or decisions and undermine your credibility as a writer.

Examples of misrepresenting data

Problem	Explanation	Example
Reliance on anecdotal evidence	Relying on personal stories or isolated examples instead of comprehensive data to make or support a claim.	Relying on a single customer testimonial as evidence that a new product is effective.
Cherry-picking time frames	Selecting specific periods that support a narrative, ignoring broader context.	Showcasing stock performance during a short market upswing, neglecting an overall downward trend.
Correlation implied as causation	Suggesting, without evidence, that because two variables correlate, one causes the other.	Suggesting that because ice cream sales and swimming pool usage go up in the same time periods, eating ice cream causes swimming pool use.
Data dredging	Searching through data to find any possible correlation without hypothesis, leading to spurious relationships.	Highlighting the correlation between the number of people who drowned by falling into a pool and the number of films featuring Nicolas Cage that premiered in a particular year.
False precision	Presenting data with unjustifiably precise figures to give an unwarranted impression of accuracy and reliability.	Claiming a project will deliver a 7.342% return on investment, suggesting unwarranted precision.
Improper scale or axis manipulation	Using graphs with truncated axes or irregular scales to exaggerate differences.	Using a bar graph with a y-axis that begins at 90% instead of 0% to make a change seem more impressive than it is.
Misleading percentages	Presenting percentages without actual numbers, creating a skewed perspective.	Claiming a "50% increase in customer satisfaction" when the increase is only from two to three respondents.

Problem	Explanation	Example
Omitting uncertainty	Not acknowledging the margin of error or uncertainty in data collection and analysis.	Presenting survey results as absolute facts without mentioning the margin of error or the response rate.
Overgeneralization	Drawing broad conclusions from limited or specific data.	Concluding that a product is a market leader based on a selective customer survey from a single region.
Selective reporting	Highlighting data that supports an argument while ignoring contradicting evidence.	Reporting on a single quarter of exceptional revenue growth while ignoring longer-term trends of declining sales.
Using raw numbers instead of ratios	Presenting raw numbers rather than numbers as a proportion of a total.	Saying "10,000 people experienced side effects" without stating that the figure was out of 10 million users, making the finding seem more significant than it is.

Use visuals for enhanced communication

Visual presentation of data (through charts, tables, infographics, etc.) can communicate large quantities of complex information in an easy-to-understand way, making it indispensable in business writing. Wise choice of visuals can make your writing more accessible and have a positive effect on your audience's comprehension and subsequent decision making.

Select visuals that match the message

There are various ways to use visuals to convey information and insight. Charts and tables present data in a quickly intelligible, organized fashion. Callout quotes (quotes featured in a visually distinctive way, such as in a larger type size) and infographics highlight specific perspectives in a concise, compelling and engaging manner.

Options for conveying data or information effectively

Type	Why	Comments
Charts	To visually simplify complex data, allowing quick comprehension of trends, comparisons and relationships.	Have clear labeling and provide contextual explanations. Use charts for data that benefits from visual representation of trends or comparisons, such as profits over time or comparisons of competitors.
Callout quotes or factoids	To emphasize key insights, provide visual breaks and reinforce messages without disrupting the narrative flow.	Strategically select quotes and factoids for stand-alone value and relevance. Place them to highlight key points. Always attribute quotes clearly.

Type	Why	Comments
Infographics	To transform complex information into engaging visual stories, increasing accessibility and engagement.	Be relevant and clear. Include descriptive text for accessibility. Introduce each infographic in the text to guide readers on its significance.
Tables	To organize detailed data in an accessible, easy-to-compare format when precision is crucial.	Use tables for detailed information requiring comparison or specific attention. Guide the reader with a brief narrative or key takeaways.

Align design decisions with your message and audience

Choice of typeface, fonts, colors, margins and layout for business documents should not be an afterthought: these choices affect readability, can enhance or undermine your message and captivate—or annoy—your audience. As you finalize a document, scrutinize the visual effect of the layout, the strategic use of imagery and the selection of colors and fonts. These choices should adhere to your organization's branding guidelines for a cohesive identity across communications and serve to reinforce the document's core message.

Guidance on key aspects of document design

Element	Guidance	Example
Audience-centric design	Design should reflect the preferences and expectations of the intended audience.	A proposal for a youth theater group using vibrant colors and dynamic layouts; a corporate strategy report in muted tones with a structured format.
Color and typography	Typefaces and colors have associations: some are seen as more conservative, others as more free-wheeling. Choose accordingly.	A professional report using a blue color scheme for trust and a serif (i.e., more conservative) typeface.
Consistency throughout	Use the same logo, color palette and typography across the document.	A document using a consistent color theme and featuring the company logo in the same location on each page.
Visual data assets	Use high-quality, relevant images to enhance the document. Use charts and infographics to simplify complex data.	A chart showing reduction in carbon emissions and a photo of a solar farm.
Photographs and icons	Use photographs or icons that align with the content and align with your reader's expectations.	Photos of individuals going through an obstacle course in a report about the challenges in risk management.
Thoughtful layout	Use white space, headings and bullet points for easy navigation.	A document with clear sections, each introduced by a descriptive heading and separated by ample white space.

Ultimately, the goal of good design is to complement the written content, to augment rather than detract from your message. Prior to publication, conduct a comprehensive review of your document, including the design elements, to be sure the design choices are doing what you intend them to do.

Use structural tools to enhance readability

We've already covered the fundamentals of structure: how to organize your thoughts, whether on the scale of the entire document or individual sentences in a paragraph. Now we'll look at tools such as headings and lists that can reinforce and enhance that structure.

Use headings and subheadings to signpost structure

Headings and subheadings serve as signposts within your document, breaking up text into digestible, related sections and highlighting key points. Your top-level headings should be the most general; subheadings under each heading should reflect topics that all belong under that heading. If a subheading has subheadings of its own, the same rule applies. Headings, subheadings and sub-subheadings form an outline for your document. They need to be crafted with care.

Headings and subheadings can be complete sentences (as most of the ones in this book are), phrases or even single words. However, all subheadings under a given heading must use the same syntax. This guarantees a parallel structure that is harmonious and aids in understanding.

Example 1

Important points when giving a speech **[heading]**

    maintaining good posture **[subheading]**

    speaking clearly **[subheading]**

    making eye contact **[subheading]**

In the example above, the subheadings are all phrases that start with a present participle (an "-ing" word).

Example 2

Important points when giving a speech **[heading]**

    good posture **[subheading]**

    clear delivery **[subheading]**

    eye contact **[subheading]**

In the second example, the subheadings are all modified nouns. Both types of subheadings are acceptable. What would be unacceptable would be to mix the two styles of subheading.

Below is further guidance on crafting headings and subheadings.

Guidance on using headings and subheadings

Recommendation	Guidance
Be descriptive yet concise	A heading should offer a clear preview of the section it introduces, using concise language that speaks directly to the content's focus.
Maintain consistency	Use a uniform style across all subheadings, including consistent capitalization and font, for a pleasing, easy-to-follow reading experience.
Use action-oriented language	Whenever possible, use active, vigorous phrasing to engage readers.
Vary length	Mix shorter and longer subheadings to maintain reader interest and adapt to the content's nature within each section.

If your writing will be presented on social media or websites, you should include relevant keywords in subheadings to improve how it gets picked up by search engine optimization (SEO), which in turn affects how many people see your writing.[1]

Use lists to present short, related ideas or points

The most simple lists are a string or group of items: a shopping list, for example, is a group of items you need to buy, and a list of job candidates is a group of applicants for the position. Simple lists can either be set off from the rest of the text in a column, or they can be run into the rest of the text.

Example is columnar list versus run-in list

Type of list	Example
Columnar list	When paying for groceries at the self-service counter, (1) scan and bag your items; (2) choose the "pay" icon; (3) insert your payment card; (4) select "print receipt"; (5) take your receipt and (6) pick up your groceries.
Run-in list	When paying for groceries at the self-service counter, (1) scan and bag your items; (2) choose the "pay" icon; (3) insert your payment card; (4) select "print receipt"; (5) take your receipt and (6) pick up your groceries.

[1] SEO is the practice of enhancing a website to improve its visibility on search engines like Google. It involves designing content and structure, such as including commonly searched keywords, so that the site appears higher in search results. This makes it easier for potential customers or readers to find the business or content online.

Number your list with words or numerals

The lists above are numbered lists, and the numbers are written as numerals. When your list is a set of directions or points for consideration, you can also write it using ordinal numbers ("first," "second," "third," etc.). The list of steps for paying for groceries at the self-service counter would look like this: "When paying for groceries at the self-service counter, first, scan and bag your items; second, choose the 'pay' icon; third, insert your payment card; fourth, select 'print receipt'; fifth, take the receipt and, sixth, pick up your groceries."

In place of "first," "second," "third," etc., you can also use "firstly," "secondly," "thirdly," etc. However, for long lists, numerals may be preferable, given it can sound cumbersome in words after 10.

Alternatively, use bullets for lists, not numbers

Columnar lists are often unnumbered. In such cases, they generally have other marks, collectively called bullets, to call attention to each item.

Example

New England state capitals

- Augusta (Maine)
- Boston (Massachusetts)
- Concord (New Hampshire)
- Hartford (Connecticut)
- Montpelier (Vermont)
- Providence (Rhode Island)

When lists form a complete sentence or several sentences, punctuate them correctly

The list of state capitals above needs no punctuation, but the list of steps for paying for groceries does. The simple rule is that if your list can be read as a complete sentence, it should be punctuated as one.

Guidance on punctuating lists

List type	Guideline	Example
Simple lists	No punctuation	<ul><li>Strategic planning</li><li>Market analysis</li><li>Product development</li></ul>
Each item in a list forms a complete sentence.	Punctuate each item as a sentence.	<ul><li>Strategic planning guides our goals.</li><li>Market analysis reveals opportunities.</li><li>Product development is progressing.</li></ul>

List type	Guideline	Example
Complex lists	Punctuate the sentence as if there were no bullet points. Note: you do not need a colon prior to the bullets any more than you would in a sentence. A colon is only used if the text before the colon forms a complete sentence.	The strategy encompasses ■ aligning goals through strategic planning; ■ conducting market analysis, which includes competitive research; and ■ advancing product development, centered on user needs.

When creating lists with more complex headings and contents, keep in mind the following points.

Guidance on crafting effective lists

Recommendation	Guidance
Use strong introductory statements	Start with a concise lead-in statement. **Example:** "To enhance operational efficiency, we recommend the following steps:"
Use summary words for easy scanning	If each item in the list is several sentences long, begin with a bolded summary word or phrase that captures the essence of the point, allowing for quick scanning. **Example:** "**Automate routine tasks:** New technologies allow..."
Maintain visual consistency	If you are using bullets, use the same shape and color across all bullets; if your list items are numbered, be sure the style for the numbers is consistent.
Be succinct	Limit each item to a single, focused idea to keep information clear and actionable to avoid overwhelming the reader.
Keep a parallel structure	All the items in a list should be styled syntactically the same. (See the guidance on headings, above.)

Structure data effectively in tables

Tables make it possible to present detailed data succinctly, but they should be used purposefully—be it to illustrate trends, support arguments or aid in decision making—and they shouldn't be overloaded with superfluous details. They are ideal for presenting numerical data and for making comparisons that would be cumbersome to explain textually. Refrain from using tables for information that could be more succinctly communicated in a sentence or two. Introduce each table clearly within your text, highlighting its relevance and summarizing key insights to effectively guide the reader. Make references to tables explicit in your main text (e.g., "See Table 1 for...").

The clarity and persuasive power of your table depends largely on how the data is organized within it. There are several strategies for ordering data, designed to align with your narrative's goals and the nature of the data:

■ **Ordinal ordering:** Data can be listed by rank for the relevant purpose or endeavor.

- **Alphabetical ordering:** Alphabetical ordering is an easily understood, neutral method of ordering data.

- **Ordering by importance:** If there is a shared sense of order of importance, then organizing data by importance prioritizes the information that people most need to see.

- **Ordering conceptually:** Tabular data can be presented based on conceptual categories (e.g., levels of maturity) or theories.

- **Ordering by observed data:** Data can be ordered based on observed patterns or relationships.

- **Ordering by survey questions:** When data from a survey is being presented, the survey questions can serve as the ordering principle.

- **Mixed ordering for complex data:** For intricate datasets, a combination of ordering principles may be used.

Appendix 3 provides a more detailed exploration of each of these methods for ordering data.

Guidance on designing compelling tables

Recommendation	Guidance
Be clear	Write clear, intelligible column and row headings, and employ logical data organization (see above).
Be concise	Use succinct phrasing and direct language within tables. Long explanations should stay in the main text.
Enhance legibility	Be generous with white space in each cell of your table so the data can be easily viewed and does not appear cramped.
Maintain uniformity	Be consistent in font, alignment and color choices across all tables in your document. This uniformity demonstrates professionalism.

Elevate your stories with charts

Charts (and diagrams and graphs; the terms are overlapping and don't have firm definitional boundaries) are another visual way of presenting information, and often they are less visually daunting than tables. A pie chart with an impressive two-thirds in one color, with other slices mere slivers, conveys the power of that proportion more than words can do.

One way to think about charts is in terms of their form: a bar chart is a set of bars; a pie chart is a circle divided into slices like a pie; a line charts shows one or several lines plotted on a field defined by x and y axes. But another way to think about charts is in terms of why they are being used.

Guidance on charts by task

Task	Example chart and use
To make a comparison	Bar charts are good for comparisons of snapshot data (e.g., comparing three companies' sales in a given year).
To show correlation	Scatter plots are good for showing a relationship between variables (e.g., between advertising spend and sales growth).
To show a part-whole relationship or a hierarchy	Pie charts are iconic for showing the relationship of parts to a whole (e.g., market share among competitors); treemaps are good for visualizing product sales by category hierarchy.
To show change over time	Line charts show change in a variable over time (e.g., a company's revenue growth); Gantt charts are useful for project management.
To show a distribution	Histograms are specialized bar charts in which each bar represents a range. They are used to show distributions (e.g., distribution of customer ages).
To show geospatial information or flow	Geographic heatmaps can be used to visualize population density, income concentration, land use, etc.; Sankey diagrams show flows from one place or state to another (e.g., resource allocation flows).

As you consider what type of chart to use to present your data, keep in mind that your choice should take into account the complexity of the data and your audience's level of expertise in addition to the factors highlighted in the guidance above.

* * * * *

Now that you have a firm grasp of the principles of good writing and data presentation, we'll turn to some special topics to further refine your business writing skills.

PART

4

Special Topics in Business Writing

This section will give you the tools you need for adding professional polish to your business writing. It provides a guide to the strategic use of acronyms and abbreviations, the inclusion of sidebars and how to gain authority through direct quotations, properly attributed. You will also learn rules for capitalization of proper nouns (names of people, places and organizations) and how to handle numbers. Lastly, this section covers references, citations and appendices, which can enhance readers' trust and secure your place as a respected source of information.

In Part 4

- Use acronyms and abbreviations to avoid repetition.
- Use sidebars to supplement the main text.
- Use quotes and quotation marks accurately.
- Understand the rules for capitalization.
- When citing numbers, keep accuracy and comprehension foremost in mind.
- Support your main report with citations, references and appendices.

Use acronyms and abbreviations to avoid repetition

Strategic use of acronyms and abbreviations can make writing much less cumbersome. Using "CDC" is less burdensome than writing out "Centers for Disease Control and Prevention," and referring to the board of directors as "the board" saves space.

Some abbreviations, like "Mr." for "mister" and "Dr." for "doctor," need no explanation: they are familiar to everyone. But in general, it is good practice to introduce any acronym or abbreviation you intend to use by giving the full name, followed by the shortened form in parentheses (you don't need to put the abbreviated term in quotation marks). From then on, you can use the shortened form. In lengthy documents, a periodic reminder of an acronym's meaning if it hasn't come up recently may enhance reader comprehension (i.e., once again write out the full name and give the acronym in parentheses after it). The inclusion of a glossary can also be helpful, especially if your document contains many acronyms.

There will no doubt be some acronyms that you decide are too familiar to warrant explanation. It's a good idea to keep a list of these and to keep it short. In a business setting, you might decide, for example, that CEO, HR and IT can be used without explanation. The primary aim is to make your writing accessible and engaging. Your goal should always be to clarify rather than obscure your message.

- **Introducing an acronym:** "According to the Environmental Protection Agency **(EPA)**, we must..."
- **Introducing an abbreviation:** "The board of directors **(board)** convened to finalize the decision."

Use "e.g." and "i.e." correctly

Mixing up "e.g." and "i.e." is common, but once you understand their meanings, it is easy to use them correctly. The first, "e.g.," comes from the Latin "exempli gratia" and means "for example."

- **Sentence using "e.g.":** "Cyber threats come in many forms (**e.g.**, malware, ransomware, phishing)."
- **Meaning:** "Cyber threats come in many forms (for example, malware, ransomware, phishing)."

The second, "i.e.," comes from the Latin "id est" and translates as "that is," meaning "in other words." It's used when what follows is a replacement for what came before.

- **Sentence using "i.e.":** "The CEO (**i.e.**, Ms. Jones) reportedly approved the appointment."
- **Meaning:** "The CEO (in other words, Ms. Jones) reportedly approved the appointment.

If you are giving an example, use "e.g." If you are restating something, use "i.e."

Employ "etc." to abbreviate lists

The abbreviation "etc." comes from the Latin "et cetera" and means "and so on." It's handy for suggesting additional items exist beyond those mentioned, especially when listing them all is unnecessary or excessive. In formal contexts, opting to write out "and so on" is an alternative. (There are other phrases, such as "among others" in the example below.) When a sentence ends with "etc.," the period at the end of the abbreviation does double duty as the sentence-final period.

- **Inappropriate use:** "Our company's values include integrity, innovation, respect, **etc.**" Here, using "etc." suggests lack of interest in the particular values the company has chosen. Furthermore, beyond the fact that the values chosen are all positive, there is no way to know what values the "and so on" represented by "etc." might encompass. The wording "among others" is less dismissive than "etc." and would be appropriate in this case. "Our company's values include integrity, innovation and respect, among others."

- **Appropriate use:** "The project requires various resources, such as paper, pens, staplers, **etc.**" Here readers can understand the type of resource being discussed and don't need an exhaustive list. They understand, for example, that other resources might include erasers or paper clips but not cake icing or railroad spikes.

Note that if you use "e.g." in your writing, you do not need to put "etc." at the end of the list; it's implied.

Write out "versus" in most cases

In discursive writing, you should spell out the word "versus" rather than abbreviating it. In tables and charts, you can use the abbreviation "vs." However, for legal cases (e.g., *Brown v. the Board of Education*), the abbreviation "v." is used. Note that British English punctuation style is to have "vs" or "v" without the period.

Avoid acronym pitfalls

While acronyms and abbreviations can make communication more efficient, you want to be careful to avoid the following common pitfalls so that your message remains clear and accessible to your audience.

Common pitfalls in using acronyms and abbreviations

Common pitfall	Problem	Recommendation
Overuse in initial introduction	Can overwhelm readers.	Space out acronym introductions in your writing and only use those essential to your narrative.
Assumption of knowledge	Some readers may not know certain acronyms.	Always spell out the full term upon first use, even if it seems widely recognized.
Inconsistent use	Can cause confusion.	Only introduce an acronym if you intend to use it. Once introduced, it should be used in preference to the full term unless there has been considerable text since last it was used. In that case, as discussed earlier, you can reintroduce it.

Common pitfall	Problem	Recommendation
Multiple new acronyms in a sentence	Create confusion.	Avoid introducing multiple new acronyms in one sentence so as to avoid a forest of confusing parentheses. If you are going to be introducing the instant messaging system AIM, for example, make sure you've introduced the acronym AOL earlier. **Weak structure:** "The messaging system from America Online (AOL), AOL Instant Messenger (AIM), was widely used in the first decade of the 21st century." **Preferable structure:** "America Online (AOL) was a powerful force in the early days of the internet. Its popular instant messenger system, AOL Instant Messenger (AIM), was widely used in the first decade of the 21st century."
Identical acronyms for different terms	Create ambiguity.	Do not use identical acronyms for different terms. Find a different way to refer to one of the terms, or write out one of the terms.
Too many acronyms; glossary overload	Too many acronyms, even if they are all listed in a glossary, can be overwhelming.	Limit your use of acronyms to ones that are truly necessary, and limit acronyms included in the glossary to those readers are likely to need to look up (e.g., even accountants may want a refresher on what PCAOB stands for, but probably no readers will need to look up IT in the glossary).

Use sidebars to supplement the main text

Sidebars are a powerful feature in business documents, offering a way to enrich the narrative with detailed explanations, case studies or data without disrupting the flow of the primary text. Visual distinction is essential. Use a unique design, background color or shading to distinguish sidebars from the main content to catch the reader's attention. You can give sidebars borders or place them in boxes to create a visual separation, and you can employ bold or larger fonts for sidebar titles. Position sidebars adjacent to relevant sections so that readers can seamlessly access additional insights without navigating away from their current reading point.

Guidance on effective ways to use sidebars

Focus	Guidance
Clarify complex concepts	Use sidebars to break down intricate ideas or processes, providing a detailed exploration that complements the main discussion.
Define terms	Offer definitions for technical jargon or industry-specific terms, aiding comprehension without overloading the main text.
Feature expert opinions	Elevate your content by including quotes or insights from industry experts, adding credibility and depth.
Offer advice	Provide actionable tips or recommendations, directly addressing the reader's potential needs or questions.

Focus	Guidance
Present data	Include statistical information or research findings to support your arguments while keeping the main text streamlined.
Showcase real-world applications	Highlight case studies or examples that demonstrate the practical application of theories or strategies discussed in your document.

Use quotes and quotation marks accurately

Using quotes in business writing is a balancing act between adding emphasis and clarity and maintaining narrative momentum. As for quotation marks, not only are they used to indicate a direct quote from someone, they are also used to correctly style titles of certain types of written work and, in some cases, to call attention to a word or phrase.

Some modification of direct quotes is permitted

Quotes can enrich business writing by lending credibility and emphasis. When you include a direct quote (i.e., someone's verbatim words as opposed to a paraphrase or indirect quote), you must use quotations marks, and the quote must be exactly what the speaker said—with the exceptions described below.

- **Direct quote:** Tony Stark said, "I am Iron Man."
- **Paraphrase (indirect quote):** Tony Stark said he was Iron Man.

Certain small changes are permitted even with direct quotes. In actual speech, people hesitate, use filler sounds like "um" and "uh" and sometime repeat words or make minute corrections. These don't need to be represented.

- **Original Taylor Swift quote on the Graham Norton Show, July 19, 2023:** "Umm, basically, I was-I was auditioning for two roles in *Les Mis*…"
- **Modified quote:** Taylor Swift said, "Basically, I was auditioning for two roles in *Les Mis*."

When you are quoting from a textual version of someone's spoken remarks or from someone's written statement, if you want to focus your quote and leave out a portion of what the person has said, use ellipses points to indicate where you have made cuts.

- **Steve Jobs, in his Stanford University Commencement Speech, June 14, 2005:**

  "Your time is limited, so don't waste it living someone else's life. Don't be trapped by dogma—which is living with the results of other people's thinking. Don't let the noise of others' opinions drown out your own inner voice. And most important, have the courage to follow your heart and intuition. They somehow already know what you truly want to become. Everything else is secondary."

- **Shortened quote for use in a document:**

  "Your time is limited … Have the courage to follow your heart and intuition."

As can be seen in the reduced Steve Jobs quote, it is permissible to make changes in capitalization without noting them. In other words, if, as in the example above, you start part of your quotation in the middle of the source sentence, use a capital letter as if the sentence began there. There is no need to indicate the change in capitalization in brackets except in legal documents. (If you were quoting Jobs in a legal document, you would write "Your time is limited ... [H]ave the courage to follow your heart and intuition.")

If you make other changes in wording, however (e.g., to explain a term when the source material used an acronym), that change should be enclosed in square brackets. Do not use parentheses (round brackets) because the reader may misinterpret that to mean the parenthetical material is part of the original quote.

- **Source quote:** "We have the best CISO in the industry."

- **Modified quote:** "We have the best CISO **[chief information security officer]** in the industry." (Note: because here you are adding explanatory information in a quote, the explanation comes after the acronym, contrary to the usual process for introducing acronyms discussed in the section on acronyms, above.)

If there is an error in your source material, you can use "sic" in square brackets to make it clear that the error was present in the source material and not a result of poor transcription.

- "We anticipate an **incrase [sic]** in sales this quarter."

Punctuate quotations correctly for different situations

The rules for punctuating quotations vary by country. The following rules apply in the United States and are widely used elsewhere in the world. However, if you are writing in a specifically British, Australian or other non-US English environment, the practice may be to use single quotation marks rather than double quotation marks for a quotation, and where you place sentence-final punctuation can vary. The style guide of *The Economist* has a comparison of some of the differences. (See additional discussion in Appendix 2.)

Note: Examples in this book are given, by default, in quotation marks. If you look back, you will see that all the example sentences or phrases are in quotation marks. However, in this section on quotations, the example sentences are not in quotation marks: only the spoken parts are in quotation marks. This is to avoid confusion regarding use of single and double quotation marks (see "Get the double and single quotation marks right for a quotation within a quotation" below).

Know the various forms for a quotation introduced by a dialogue tag ("said," "remarked," "asked," etc.)

If the quotation is introduced by a dialogue tag, the first word of the quotation is capitalized. There's a comma after the dialogue tag and before the opening quotation marks. If the quotation represents the end of a sentence, then it ends with sentence-final punctuation (a period, question mark or exclamation point), followed by the closing quotation marks. If the sentence continues after the quotation, a comma replaces the period before the closing quotation marks (question marks and exclamation points do not change).

- **Sentence ends with the quotation (period):** The CEO said, "Innovation drives our success."

- **Sentence ends with the quotation (question mark):** The CEO asked, "Will the board support this initiative?"

- **Sentence continues after the quotation (comma):** The CEO said, "Innovation drives our success," and the audience applauded.

- **Sentence continues after the quotation (question mark):** The CEO asked, "Will the board support this initiative?" and board members glanced at each other uneasily.

Get capitalization and punctuation right for a quotation followed by a dialogue tag

If the quotation is followed by a dialogue tag, the first word of the quotation is capitalized. The quote ends with either a comma, question mark or exclamation point, followed by the closing quotation marks, and then the dialogue tag.

- **Example (comma):** "Our focus is on sustainable growth," said the CEO.
- **Example (exclamation point):** "Not on my watch!" declared the CEO.

Know the various forms for a quotation that runs into the text without a dialogue tag

If the quotation is run into the text, capitalization and punctuation follow the rules for an ordinary sentence. The first word of the quotation is only capitalized if the quote begins the sentence. If the quotation ends the sentence, generally, the sentence-final punctuation is inside the quotation marks.

- **Quotation starts the sentence:** "Live without regrets" is advice that's easier to give than to practice.
- **Quotation in the middle of the sentence:** His mentor's advice to "live without regrets" echoed in his mind.
- **Quotation at the end of the sentence:** On death's door, he was satisfied he had followed his mentor's advice to "live without regrets."

There is an exception to the placement of punctuation at the end of a sentence: if the quote is declarative but the sentence that it's contained in is a question or an exclamation, the question mark or exclamation point go outside the quotation marks.

- **Exception:** Is it really possible to "live without regrets"?

Get the double and single quotation marks right for a quotation within a quotation

In the United States, double quotation marks are used for a quotation and single quotation marks are used for quotations within quotations. (The reverse is generally true in British English.) The same rules of punctuation apply as for a simple quotation (i.e., not one that is a quotation within a quotation).

- **Example:** "I heard her say, 'This is a critical juncture for our company,'" reported the director.

Indent quotation that is more than four lines or so long

For longer quotes, the entire quotation should be set as an indented block of text, without quotation marks. Capitalization and punctuation are as they would be for an ordinary run-in quotation. As with lists, a colon should only be used if what precedes it is a complete sentence, as in the second example.

- The final report stated that

    the integration of innovative technologies has not only streamlined operations but also significantly enhanced client satisfaction across all service sectors. This paradigm shift, while challenging to implement, offers a tangible competitive advantage in the rapidly evolving digital landscape.

- The CEO highlighted a key point in the final report:

    The integration of innovative technologies has not only streamlined operations but also significantly enhanced client satisfaction across all service sectors. This paradigm shift, while challenging to implement, offers a tangible competitive advantage in the rapidly evolving digital landscape.

In dialogue, start a new paragraph each time the speaker changes

In English-speaking countries, it's a convention of representing dialogue in print to start a new paragraph each time the speaker changes, as shown here:

"Our financial outlook is robust," the CFO said. He flashed a series of charts on the screen, each showing gains and growth.

"That's excellent news," the CEO replied.

Use the correct styling for titles of works

Titles of books and plays and names of journals, magazines and newspapers are put in italics. Articles in journals, magazines and newspapers are put in quotation marks, as are titles of chapters in books and titles of most poems. Conventions around stand-alone reports (such as white papers) vary: you can choose to italicize them or put them in quotation marks, but be consistent. If you put one white paper in quotation marks, you should put all white papers in quotation marks; if you use italics, the same. Conventions related to using italics or quotation marks to cite material available on the web vary, as well: your goal should be consistency in treatment.

Examples of titles to put in italics:

- *To Kill a Mockingbird* (book title)

- *Romeo and Juliet* (play)

- *Marketing Science* (journal title)

- *Fortune* (magazine title)

- *The Wall Street Journal* (newspaper title) Note: some style guides include "The" in the title of the newspaper and therefore italicize it; others do not.

Examples of titles to put in quotation marks:

- "Why Labor Supply Matters for Macroeconomics" (article in the Spring 2024 issue of *Journal of Economic Perspectives*)

- "Inside Volkswagen's $130 Billion EV Battle" (article in the August 1, 2024, issue of *Fortune*)

- "WSJ Reporter Evan Gershkovich Is Free" (article in the August 1, 2024, issue of *The Wall Street Journal*)

- "Rainbow Economics: Closing the Racial Wealth Divide" (chapter in the book *The Color of Wealth: The Story Behind the U.S. Wealth Divide*)

- "Where the Sidewalk Ends" (poem in the collection *Where the Sidewalk Ends: Poems and Drawings*)

When you have a title in quotation marks in running text, a period or comma goes inside the closing quotation mark, and a question mark or exclamation point goes after the closing quotation mark (unless the question mark or exclamation point is part of the title).

Examples:

- The reporter, having decided she would ask Mark Zuckerberg if he had ever read the poem "Where the Sidewalk Ends," eagerly raised her hand.

- Has Mark Zuckerberg ever read the poem "Where the Sidewalk Ends"?

Use quotes to introduce unfamiliar terms, but do not use them for emphasis

When you are introducing a specialized or technical term that may be new or unfamiliar to your readers, putting the term in quotation marks is a good way to call attention to it. An explanation should follow, after which you should no longer put quotation marks around the word. It's important to limit this use of quotation marks to terms that are truly likely to be unfamiliar.

- **Correct use of quotation marks to introduce a specialized term:** The enthusiasm for **"cottagecore,"** an aesthetic celebrating rural life, skyrocketed during the COVID-19 pandemic.

Note that the term is defined. Henceforward, it should be used without quotation marks.

Quotation marks should never be used just to emphasize a word. Care should also be taken in using quotation marks to highlight an ironic, sarcastic or somehow nonstandard use of a word. Quotation marks used this way are called "scare quotes." Putting ordinary, familiar words in quotation marks risks readers thinking you are using the word ironically or sarcastically.

- **Incorrect use of quotation marks to stress a word:** What distinguishes us from the competition is our **"innovation"**: we are trendsetters in plumbing seals.

Quotation marks around "innovation" will make the reader think that the word is being used in an ironic, sarcastic or nonstandard way, which is not what the writer wants.

- **Deliberate use of quotation marks for sarcasm:** The tutor's **"study"** methods included instructions on how to steal an advance copy of the exam.

Stealing an advance copy of the exam is not a proper study method, hence this usage is ironic—a correct use of scare quotes.

Understand the rules for capitalization

Capitalized words have special significance. In English we capitalize proper nouns (names of people, places and organizations or entities) and words associated with proper nouns, including titles. There are also rules for capitalization of titles of works.

Capitalize proper nouns and titles correctly

We capitalize proper nouns, and we capitalize titles when used in conjunction with a proper noun. Titles are not capitalized, however, when they are used alone.

- "**President Ronald Reagan** will address the issue." (Titles used with names are capitalized.)
- "I spoke with the **president** yesterday." (Titles are not capitalized when they are not used with names.)

When a title is used in place of a name or as a form of address, it is capitalized.

- "The event was for **grandmothers** only." (The word "grandmother" is not capitalized.)
- "I spoke with **Grandmother** about the event." (In this instance "grandmother" is used in place of a name.)

Compass directions and geographic features are lowercased unless they are part of a name.

- "Go **west** for three miles." (Compass directions are not capitalized.)

- "They moved to **West Virginia**." ("West Virginia" is a proper noun, so "West" is capitalized.)

- "There is a mighty **river** running through Egypt." (Geographic features are not capitalized.)

- "The **Nile River** is in Egypt." (As part of the proper noun "Nile River," the word "river" is capitalized.)

Capitalize the names of languages, nationalities and ethnic and racial groups.

- "The document was translated into **German**." (Languages are capitalized.)

- "The **Swedish** author won the prize." (Nationalities are capitalized.)

- "The company's new initiative aims to support **Black** communities through educational grants." (Racial groups are capitalized.)

Seasons are generally lowercased, but are capitalized when part of a name, title or when giving bibliographic information about journals or magazines that publish seasonally. Months and days are capitalized, as are the names of holidays.

- "We expect profits to rise in the **spring**." (Seasons are lowercased in everyday usage.)

- "The **Winter Olympics** will be televised." (Seasons are capitalized as part of a name.)

- "The **Fall edition** covered the best places to see the foliage in New England." (Seasons are capitalized when referencing specific seasonal editions of journals or magazines.)

- "The conference is scheduled for **Thursday, July 4, Independence Day**." (Days, months and holidays are capitalized.)

Choose a method for capitalizing titles of works

There are two methods for capitalizing titles of works (e.g., books, journals, articles, etc.): headline style and sentence style. Headline style capitalizes all words except conjunctions and prepositions; sentence style capitalizes only the first word, proper nouns and the first word following a colon.

In running text (i.e., when the works are mentioned within the sentence), titles of works that are styled in italics (see "Use the correct styling for titles of works," above) are always capitalized using headline style (i.e., *The Grapes of Wrath*, not *The grapes of wrath*). Works that are styled in quotation marks may be capitalized using either headline style or sentence style, depending on your preference, but be consistent.

For capitalization of works in reference lists, bibliographies and footnotes, it is simplest to use a method from an established style manual. (See Appendix 4 for guidance on citing materials using the American Psychological Association [APA] style.)

- **Headline capitalization:** "Capitalizing on the Cloud and AI: How Is Your Company Placed?" (All words are capitalized except conjunctions and prepositions.)

- **Sentence capitalization:** "Trends in renewable energy in China: A comprehensive review." (Only the first word, the proper noun and the first word after the colon are capitalized.)

When citing numbers, keep accuracy and comprehension foremost in mind

The facts don't speak for themselves, and nor do numbers. How people understand the numbers you cite depends on how you present them. You should strive for maximum comprehension. Appropriate rounding can simplify your message without sacrificing precision, but keep in mind that certain contexts require exact figures. In scenarios where specifics are crucial, your numbers should be precise to maintain the integrity and credibility of your communication.

Guidance on when approximation is appropriate

Context	Guideline	Example
Broad summaries	Approximation aids comprehension by giving readers a general sense of the situation. In these situations exact numbers can be overly fussy.	"Annual revenue was **approximately 100 million** dollars."
Noncritical estimates	Rounding to the nearest ten or hundred is practical for informal estimates.	"**About 1,900** survey responses were received."

Guidance on when exact numbers are appropriate

Context	Guideline	Example
Precise reporting	Exact figures are crucial in financial documents or contracts.	"The July 30 Form 10-Q revealed that **6,642,228 shares** were purchased between April 1 and June 3, 2024."
Scientific accuracy	Technical data or research findings require exact numbers; rounding could mislead or result in inaccuracies.	"A test found PFOA contamination of **95.9 ppt** in the municipal water supply, thousands of times higher than federal standards."

Further guidance on presenting numbers in text is offered as follows.

Guidance on expressing numbers in writing

Context	Guideline	Example
Numbers in running text	Spell out numbers zero through nine; use numerals for 10 and above. If a sentence begins with a number, write it out. Reword the sentence if the number at the beginning of the sentence is inconveniently large (e.g., "One hundred thirty protesters were arrested…" can be rephrased as "Police arrested 130 protesters…").	"At the meeting, representatives from **three** of our **10** clients were present." "**Twenty** employees were promoted last month."

Context	Guideline	Example
Placing commas in large numbers	For numbers in the thousands and above, place commas after every third multiple of 10.	**1,000** (one thousand) **1,000,000** (one million) **1,000,000,000** (one billion) Note: This is the US meaning of the word "billion," which has gained widespread use, but some English-speaking countries use "billion" to mean a million millions rather than, as here, a thousand millions. In US usage, a million millions is a trillion: 1,000,000,000,000.
Very large numbers	For extremely large or small numbers, use scientific notation.	"The universe's diameter is **8.8×10^{26} meters**."
Change in numbers	When stating a numerical change, consider the order in which you state the initial and final values. You can state the values in chronological order or put the final value first if you want to emphasize the outcome.	**Chronological order:** "The stock price fell **from $60 to $45** in just one week." **Final value first**: "The stock price dropped **to $45 from $60** in just one week."
Decimals or fractions?	Use decimals for precision in technical contexts; use spelled-out fractions for a conversational tone or approximations.	**Decimal:** "**3.75%** increase." **Fraction:** "**One-half** prefer flexible hours."
Currency	If writing for an international audience, distinguish US dollars as "US$" to avoid confusion with other dollar-denominated currencies. Convert currencies when relevant for your audience. For substantial amounts, spell out "million," "billion," or use abbreviations ("M" for million, "B" for billion).	"**US$5,000** (approximately **€4,200**)." "The company's valuation reached **US$5 billion**."
Legal contexts	Use numerals followed by spelled-out forms in parentheses in legal documents.	"**100,000 (one hundred thousand)** dollars."
Ranges	An en dash can replace "to" in a sentence with a numerical range except in cases where the range includes the word "from."	"Records show **300 to 500** people visited monthly" **OR** "Records show **300–500** people visited monthly" **BUT** "In March, **from 300 to 500** calls were logged daily." (The word "to" cannot be replaced with an en dash.)
Percentages	Use numerals and spell out "percent" in formal contexts; use "%" in less formal contexts or for brevity (e.g., in tables).	**Formal:** "**75 percent** agree." **Informal:** "The solution contains **5%** salt."

Context	Guideline	Example
Exact numbers, approximations and estimates	Use exact numbers when precision is warranted, or when approximation provides no benefit over exact numbers. Use approximation when a general sense is desired and exact numbers would be spurious. When a number is approximate, indicate that fact with words such as "approximately," "about," "nearly" or "just over." Use similar words for denoting estimates.	**Exact number:** "The town voted down funding for the new school by a vote of **2,539 to 1,548**." **Approximation**: "In August 2024, the US population was **approximately 336.8 million**." **Estimate:** "Organizers estimated **about 20,000** people attend the event."
Time notation accuracy	Use "a.m." and "p.m." with periods and lowercase letters for formal business writing.	"The meeting is at **10:30 a.m.**"
Dates	In the US, dates are typically written in month-day-year format. Internationally, day-month-year format is more common. For US-format dates, if dates appear in the middle of a sentence, place a comma after the day and after the year (i.e., the year is set off by commas). For international-format dates, no commas are needed within the day-month-year format, but a comma may be needed after the date, depending on sentence structure. In general, select the format aligned to the place of publication, unless an adopted style guide says otherwise.	**Full date:** ■ **US:** February 24, 1997 ■ **International:** 24 February 1997 **Numeric date:** ■ **US**: 02/24/1997 ■ **International:** 24/2/1997 **In sentence:** ■ **US:** "On **February 24, 1997**, the wedding took place." ■ **International:** "On **24 February 1997**, the wedding took place."

Support your main report with citations, references and appendices

Citations, either in the form of footnotes or endnotes (collectively known as "notes") or in the form of in-text citations and a reference list, bolster your credibility by showing readers you consulted multiple sources to arrive at your ideas. They also provide readers with a means to do pursue more information themselves, should they want to. Appendices, for their part, give you the opportunity to provide supporting information and additional context. These tools can be beneficial, but they also can interfere with the reading experience and are not always necessary. You have to determine whether or not they are appropriate for your writing project.

Each form of citation has advantages and disadvantages

Footnotes appear at the bottom of each page, which allows readers to quickly glance down and find the bibliographic information on the work you're citing. However, if footnotes become too copious, they can end up taking up a lot of page space and distract the reader. Endnotes, located at the end of the document or chapter, keep the main text uncluttered, but they require the reader to flip back and forth in order to read them. This is less of a problem with electronic documents, which can send the reader to an endnote through a hyperlink, but if your document will have physical form, you should bear in mind this drawback of endnotes.

The advantage of using in-text citations and a reference list as a method of citation is that it alerts readers right in the main text to the sources you have consulted in the form of the author(s) names and the publication year. Readers can then consult the reference list for the complete bibliographic information on the source. This method gives readers more information in the main text than the note system without being overly distracting. The disadvantage is that as with endnotes, this system requires readers to go to a different location in the document for complete information.

Guidance on how to format notes and reference list entries is offered in Appendix 4. Samples of in-text citations are shown below.

Examples:

- (Smith, 2022)

- (Smith & Jones, 2023)

- (Centers for Disease Control and Prevention, 2021)

Use footnotes and endnotes to provide other sorts of information

In addition to being one method for citing sources, notes are used for providing certain types of information that don't fit into the main flow of the text. Even if you are using in-text citations and a reference list to cite the works you have consulted, you can use notes (either footnotes or endnotes) to provide these types of information.

Guidance on content can be relegated to footnotes and endnotes

Content	Guidance	Example
Acknowledgments or credits	Many times a report or paper will have a special acknowledgments statement at the beginning or end, but sometimes you may want to make a particular acknowledgment. This type of acknowledgment can go in a note.	"This framework was developed in collaboration with the R&D department."
Information on source data	Details about the source, year and context of your data can go in a note.	"This analysis relies on data from the 2022 Global Market Survey by XYZ Research."
A tangential insight or commentary	On occasion you may have an additional insight to offer that is not directly related to the discussion at hand. If it's truly worth including, then it can go in a note.	"Interestingly, this trend can also be noted in such unrelated fields as commercial fishing and early childhood education. See Ishikawa, N. (2023), The scarcity factor," *Kaleidoscope Journal* 2(4), 15–32."
Definitions	If it's inconvenient to interrupt the flow of the discussion in your main text, you can put definitions of unfamiliar terms in a note.	"EBITDA stands for 'earnings before interest, taxes, depreciation, and amortization.'"

Content	Guidance	Example
Legal or regulatory references	Provide specific legal text or regulation numbers in a note.	"See Section 4, Paragraph 2 of the Consumer Data Protection Act (2018)."
Methodology explanation	If the explanation is brief, you can provide it in a note. If it's longer, then an appendix is a better choice.	"The survey was conducted across 10 countries, with over 5,000 participants from various industries."

Use appendices selectively to expand on key points

Appendices are a strategic element of business documents, designed to house supplementary material in a way that enhances the main text without overburdening it. Do not relegate information that is crucial to the document's main argument or narrative to an appendix. If the reader needs the information to follow your main points, integrate it into the main text.

While it may be tempting to include multiple appendices to encompass all available information, exercise restraint. Appendices shouldn't be used for indiscriminate sharing; they should serve a specific purpose, such as deepening understanding, providing necessary verification or facilitating further exploration. Choose materials that contribute substantive value to the document and keep them succinct.

Guidance on effective uses of appendices

Use	Description
Legal documents or references	Full texts of referenced legal documents, technical standards or materials that provide essential context or compliance information.
Methodological details	Crucial details for understanding how a study was conducted or how it could be replicated.
Supporting data	Datasets, research findings or complex tables that support the document's arguments.
Supplementary information	Detailed background information, technical specifications or extended case studies that are relevant.

Guidance on designing appendices

Best practice	Guidance
Brief introduction	Include a brief introduction at the beginning of each appendix, explaining its relevance and summarizing its contents. **Example:** "This appendix provides the datasets supporting our market analysis."

Best practice	Guidance
Well organized	Appendices should be as easy to navigate as the main document, with clear headings and logical flow of information. Number or letter each appendix and provide a descriptive title for easy navigation and reference (e.g., "Appendix A: Annual Sales Data (2015-2020)" followed by "Appendix B: Technical Specifications").
Consistently formatted	Format and style should be consistent with the main document (same fonts, same point size for comparable headings, same spacing between paragraphs).
Referenced in main text	Each appendix must be clearly referenced in the main text. **Example:** "For a comprehensive breakdown of the data analysis methods employed, refer to Appendix D."

* * * * *

You've now broadened your knowledge to include correct ways to use acronyms and quotations. You can now express numbers in ways that are suitable for your text, and capitalization no longer confuses you. You understand how to present supplementary material in sidebars, appendices or, on occasion, notes, and you know how to support your work and enhance your trustworthiness through citations. Now it's time to refine your drafts. In the next section, we'll dive into editing and revising, where you'll learn to polish your work to perfection, raising your business writing from effective to exceptional.

PART

5

Refining Your Draft

This section is dedicated to the art and science of editing, a critical phase where your draft transforms into a polished masterpiece. Here, we examine time-tested editing strategies, highlight common pitfalls and show how to harness feedback to refine your prose. Editing is not just about correction; it's an opportunity to learn and adapt your style, making your writing more clear, precise

In Part 5

- Employ time-tested editing strategies.
- Use a checklist to help eliminate common mistakes.
- Integrate feedback insights.
- Think of improvement as a continuous journey.

> "To me, rewriting is the most exciting part of the process."
>
> — Judy Blume, author

Employ time-tested editing strategies

Editing is an essential skill that requires a blend of patience, attention to detail and strategic application of proven techniques.

Guidance on editing strategies

Strategy	Explanation and application
Read through your draft several times	Some checks don't require a complete reread: for those, see "Use checklists," below. But to get a sense of overall flow, catch repetitions and notice oversights, you will need to do a complete read-through.
Read your draft aloud	Reading your text aloud can expose awkward phrasing, repetition and clarity issues. It mimics the reader's internal voice and helps catch errors silent reading might overlook.
Strategically pause	Taking a break after completing a first draft allows you to return with a fresh perspective, crucial for catching errors and making improvements. For short projects, aim for at least a few hours away; for bigger projects, a day—or longer, if possible—away from your writing will keep you from missing things due to overfamiliarity.
Use checklists	Use detailed checklists to address such aspects of writing as capitalization (have you been careful to lowercase "president" when it's used alone and to capitalize it when it's part of a personal title or a form of address?), punctuation (have you punctuated your quotations correctly?), word use (have you used that one word too many times?), etc. This systematic approach enables consistency and thoroughness in editing. (See the following section for more details.)
Solicit feedback	Ask peers to read your work and give you feedback, and then consider what they say. Do they appear to understand your arguments? Is there anything that confused them? If you have particular concerns, you can ask questions to direct their attention to those areas. (See the section on integrating feedback for more details.)

Strategy	Explanation and application
Use editing tools	Employ digital tools for grammar checking, style guidance and readability improvement. But remember, while these can be highly effective in identifying technical errors, they can make mistakes, especially with complex sentences. They should complement, not replace, careful human editing.

Use a checklist to help eliminate common mistakes

Let's examine one of the techniques from the guidance above in more detail: using checklists. Common issues that can detract from the quality of business writing can be categorized into three areas, each critical to crafting a compelling, professional document:

- **Style improvements:** Aim for clarity and engagement by activating your voice and eliminating redundancy.

- **Grammatical corrections:** Improve your intelligibility by checking for verb tense consistency and correct punctuation.

- **Formatting adjustments:** The presentation of your writing is as crucial as its content. Strive for visual harmony through consistent styling and orderly formatting.

The following checklist highlights specific mistakes to watch for in each category and offers practical solutions to refine your business prose effectively.

Illustrative editing checklist

Refine your style	Correct grammar errors	Check formatting
- Check for undo passive voice; substitute active voice. - Cut unnecessary repetition. - Be sure your pronouns clearly refer to the correct words. - Correct misused words: (e.g., affect/effect). - Be sure your modifiers are modifying the correct thing. - Remove superfluous adverbs (e.g., "very unique"). - Replace generalities with specific details. - Replace clichés and jargon with clear, accessible language. - Break up long paragraphs. - Explain unfamiliar terms and acronyms.	- Remove unnecessary articles (e.g., "Data shows," not "The data shows"). - Maintain uniform verb tenses throughout. - Maintain subject-verb agreement (e.g., "The women were," not "The women was"). - Correct any run-on sentences. - Add what's missing from sentence fragments to make them complete sentences; every sentence needs a subject and verb. - Correct punctuation errors (e.g., insert a comma after "eat" in "Let's eat Grandma" to prevent cannibalistic overtones). - Search for and correct typographical errors.	- Be sure you have maintained consistent styling in your headings and subheadings. - Use a uniform bullet style and alignment. - Choose one font type and size for body text. - Use consistent line and paragraph spacing. - Use standard margins. - Stick to one format for numbers, dates and times. - Use bold and italics sparingly and consistently. - Check that tables and charts are well-integrated and clear. - Use a consistent style for references and citations.

Integrate feedback insights

Feedback is an indispensable part of the editing process: it lets you see how others understand your work. Think of it as a focus group or a test drive for your document. Embrace feedback as a learning tool that shows you where your communication skills may need strengthening. Judicious incorporation of feedback will make each subsequent piece of writing stronger and more effective. The judiciousness is key: don't thoughtlessly accept all edits from those reviewing your writing; consider the changes they suggest and why.

Guidance on benefiting most from feedback

Strategy	Approach	Example
Be open to critique	View constructive criticism as an opportunity for growth, not personal criticism.	Respond to critique with questions on how to improve, rather than defense of the original text.
Diversify your sources of feedback	Ask for feedback from a variety of sources for a well-rounded perspective.	Request feedback from a colleague for clarity, a manager for strategic alignment and a member of the target audience for relevance and engagement.
Focus your request for feedback	Guide feedback with focused questions to yield actionable insights.	Instead of asking "Is this good?" ask "Does the introduction clearly outline the objectives of the document?"
Integrate and iterate	Continuously refine your writing by incorporating feedback and revisiting the content	After receiving feedback, revise the document accordingly and potentially seek a second round of reviews to confirm improvements are effective.

"If we shield ourselves from all feedback, we stop growing."

— Brené Brown, philosopher and public speaker

Think of improvement as a continuous journey

The art of editing is where true refinement in your craft occurs. With every draft you revise, every error you correct and every piece of feedback you incorporate, you inch closer to achieving excellence in your writing. Editing is the crucible in which your ideas are purified, your arguments fortified and your unique voice honed. Embrace this journey of improvement with enthusiasm and dedication, for it is through your dedicated efforts that you enhance your current work and lay the groundwork for future achievements.

PART

6

Using AI in Business Writing

In this section, we explore how to make the most of artificial intelligence (AI) in business writing. You'll learn to craft effective prompts, use AI to develop content and structure, and refine the output into polished, powerful writing.

In Part 6

- Know how to prompt.
- Understand where to edit the weaknesses of AI-generated text.

Know how to prompt

To generate text, an AI tool like ChatGPT must be given a prompt. For example, you might start with a simple request, like, "Summarize the key benefits of remote work for employees," and the AI will generate a response based on that input. However, the response will likely be fairly broad and not fully aligned with your expectations. To refine the AI's response, treat your interaction with the AI as a conversation—just as you would refine and clarify your requests in a dialogue with a colleague. By doing so, you help the AI better understand your needs and deliver results that are more in line with your goals. Remember, AI can't read your mind; your prompts should be clear, well-structured and specific.

Be specific in your prompts

The more specific your prompt, the better the response. If you need prose for a section comparing the benefits of remote work versus hybrid work models in your report, don't just say "workplace strategies"; specify those two models. Additionally, specify the exact length (e.g., "This section should be 350–400 words, no longer or shorter"). If you prefer a particular structure, such as an opening paragraph followed by bulleted content, say so. If you want the opening paragraph to be substantive rather than a list, be clear: "Create a 3–4 sentence lead-in paragraph teeing up this section; do not simply list the topics that follow." Clarify how you want bullets written; for example, "Bullets should start with an action-oriented bold statement, followed by 3–4 tight, substantive sentences explaining the point."

Identify your audience

Specify the audience in your prompts, such as board directors, senior executives, mid-level managers or new recruits, and specify the depth of their knowledge—whether they are deeply experienced, highly technical, business-savvy but not technical, etc.

- **Example:** "Write a summary of the latest cybersecurity threats tailored for senior executives at a global financial institution. Assume they have a strong understanding of business strategy and risk management but limited technical knowledge of cybersecurity. The summary should highlight the strategic implications of these threats without delving into overly technical details."

Provide context in your request

Explain the context or background of your desired article or report and what it seeks to address. If it's an introductory text, specify that. If it's a more in-depth, technical report, request that the prose and terminology reflect that level of detail. State the intent of the piece: Is it educational? Marketing-focused? Something else?

- **Example:** "Create an educational white paper on the fundamentals of AI in healthcare, aimed at senior healthcare administrators who are exploring AI implementation for the first time. The document should cover the basic principles of AI, its current applications in healthcare (such as diagnostics, patient care and administrative efficiency) and the potential benefits and challenges. The objective is to provide a clear, accessible introduction that will help decision makers understand the strategic value of AI in healthcare. Where possible, include case studies and fact-based industry statistics (with proper citations). Don't fabricate statistics or sources. The discussion of the ethical considerations surrounding AI should be balanced."

Note: even with such a prompt, you should always verify all statistics and sources. AI can sometimes generate facts, sources or quotations that do not exist, a phenomenon known as AI hallucinations. These fabrications are not flagged, so careful verification is essential.

Influence the style of writing

Each AI tool has a default writing style. Unless you specify your desired style, the tool will default to its own. In a business context, you may want substantive, nontechnical, accessible prose. Specify this by saying something like "Write for an experienced senior executive in layman's terms." Also, mention what styles to avoid, such as "Avoid consulting jargon or flowery prose" or "Avoid clichés and hyperbole." As you continue the discussion chain, seeking content for the subsequent sections, remind the tool to sustain the style: "In the exact same style as your prior response, please..." Watch out for the style or format evolving away from what you want.

Include prior responses in prompts

AI tools can be forgetful, even within a single string of conversation. To counter this, repeat prior responses in your prompts. For example, "The current structure is below," followed by your question and the tool's previous response. This avoids misunderstanding, saves time and reduces frustration.

Ask for a revised response if unsatisfied

Some responses will be underwhelming. You have three options: (1) Simply click the "regenerate" option to get a new response to the same prompt. This is effective when the initial response is on the right track but could be improved. (2) In the subsequent prompt, indicate that you don't like the response and specify what you'd like changed. This works well when the content is generally correct but needs refinement in certain areas. (3) Edit your prompt (but before editing the prompt, save elements of the initial response you like). This is often the best approach when the initial response is significantly off from what you wanted.

Iterate to determine structure

AI tools are excellent for developing outlines for reports or articles, but the prompts you use significantly influence the quality of the structure generated. Instead of merely stating the topic, outline the general set of topics you want covered, ideally in some kind of order. Prompt the tool to suggest any additional content that could enhance the report structure.

You may need to iterate several times to achieve the desired structure, flow and content. Treat the tool as you would a colleague: praise its efforts and provide specific feedback for improvement. For example, "We seem to have missed [topic A]," "Does it make sense to cover [topic B] before [topic C]?" or "Section A seems outsized compared to the other sections—can we balance it better?" Offering positive feedback, such as "This section is well-organized and clear," helps reinforce effective patterns and encourages the tool to continue producing quality responses. Even when you're satisfied with the structure, it's useful to review the outline one last time with the AI tool. End this prompt with "Be very specific on what enhancements you would make and exactly where." Without this clarification, you might get a vague list of enhancements that are difficult to address.

- **Example (early in the iteration process):** "Draft an outline for a report on sustainable business practices. The report should cover the importance of sustainability in modern business, strategies for implementing sustainable practices and significant challenges faced in various industries. Please start with an introduction to the concept and follow it with sections on specific strategies, such as energy efficiency, waste reduction and ethical sourcing. Add any additional content you think would enhance the structure. Make each section similar in length and make the flow logical and compelling. Avoid repetition across sections."

- **Example (final review):** "Here's the final structure for our report on sustainable business practices. Does this outline hang together well? What's missing? What high-value enhancements would you recommend? Are there any fatal flaws in the structure? Be very specific on what enhancements you would make and exactly where to make them."

Ask for specific content in a sidebar

When you need a sidebar or supplementary content, be explicit about what you want covered, the style and the length. The more detailed your prompt, the better the outcome.

- **Example:** "Create a 150–200 word sidebar for our report on employee wellness programs. It should briefly outline three innovative and real wellness initiatives that companies are using today. Each initiative should be introduced with a bold, engaging headline and followed by 2–3 sentences explaining it and its benefits. The tone should be positive and forward looking, aimed at HR managers who are considering updating their wellness programs. The sidebar should avoid overly technical details but provide enough information to generate interest in these new approaches. Include suggested reading for each type of initiative to encourage further exploration."

Play back near-final content

Once you have a strong baseline, identify targeted enhancement opportunities within sections:

- **Iterate for depth:** Prompt the AI to delve deeper into each section.

  Example: "In section 2, expand on the benefits, considering short-term and long-term effects."

Refine transitions: Ask the AI to improve the transitions between sections for better flow.

Example: "Smooth the transitions between sections, especially from the topic of malware to the topic of phishing."

Once your article or report is nearing a final stage, ask the tool to review it for consistency in tone, terminology and style.

- **Example:** "Check the document for consistent use of technical terms, and maintain a uniform tone throughout."

If your completed document is longer than the tool can handle, have it check sizeable chunks to at least address uniformity across subsections. To avoid unwanted wholesale rewrites, specify, "I'm very satisfied with the following, but identify any specific changes required for consistency, providing exact prose to change and noting where to put them, and identify any fatal flaws, again providing very specific changes to address them, if any. It's OK to simply respond, 'There are no changes required and no fatal flaws.'" The last part doesn't mean the AI tool will opt to not offer suggested changes, but without it, the tool often feels obliged to do so.

Recognize when the tool has reached its limits

Know when the tool has done all that it can do and further responses will either iterate without improvement or degrade in quality. This terminal level applies to both content (where the AI starts adding information that lacks essential nuance or is erroneous) and prose style (where writing quality deteriorates). At this point, transfer the content to your preferred writing application and begin refining it manually.

Understand where to edit the weaknesses of AI-generated text

It is important to understand the limitations of AI-generated writing and be prepared to rigorously edit the output to meet your high standards of quality and readability. Use a metaphorical red pen to refine AI-generated prose, aiming for a voice and presentation that will resonate with your target readers and be true to your desired style. Keep in mind that because all AI tools have been trained on existing external content, much of which is mediocre, the prose they generate often reflects the same flaws. Strengthening your own writing abilities before employing AI means you will be able to correct for this weakness. Also be aware that if you have style preferences that are less common (for example, in your choices for punctuation, capitalization or spelling), the tool will keep trying to substitute more common options. By consistently resisting these substitutions, you help preserve your preferred style.

As a reminder: as you edit, fact-check the content for accuracy. Most AI tools flag some of the generated content as potentially wrong, and they mean it.

Potential shortcomings of AI-generated prose

Shortcoming	Description
Dull titles	Regularly uses dull two-part titles (e.g., "Writing is hard: Strategies to get going.") and routinely opts for "Navigating challenges," "Addressing a volatile environment" or similarly overused titles.
Lack of contextual understanding	Sometimes fails to grasp the broader context of the topic, leading to irrelevant or shallow content.
Inappropriate tone for audience	Sometimes adopts a tone that is either too casual or too formal for the intended audience.
Weak beginnings	Has a tendency to begin sections with monotonous or overused phrases like "In the realm of fast-paced change."
Disorganization	Faces challenges in structuring content powerfully, often resulting in a disjointed flow and lack of coherence.
Generalizations and repetitions	Makes frequent unsupported generalizations and repeats certain phrases.
Undifferentiated text blocks	May generate over 300–400 words of undifferenced prose with no visual signposting of key points (e.g., subheadings, bold text or bullets).
Ineffective bullet points	Struggles with crafting effective bullet points; its lead-in statements often lack strength and precision. The bullets can feel insubstantial.
Hyperbolic and trendy language	Habitually employs hyperbolic adjectives and trendy verbs, notably those ending in "ize."
Jargon and technical lingo	Tends to revert to corporate jargon and technical lingo, even after instructions to avoid such language.
Verbose explanations	Provides explanations that are longer than necessary.
Multisyllable verbs	Prefers multisyllable verbs like "reiterate" to simpler alternatives like "repeat."
Inconsistent terminology	Uses different terms for the same concept, leading to confusion (e.g., using "stakeholders" in one paragraph and "interested parties" in the next without clarification).
Overuse of prescriptive verbs and confusion over industry practices	Overuses "must" and "should" when formatting recommendations, overuses "ensure" when explaining what's needed and confuses prevalence of practices adopted in industry (e.g., mixing up "best practice" and "good practice").
Unnecessary articles and filler words	Inserts unnecessary articles ("the," "a," "an") and filler words (e.g., "both," "very," "that"), making the text wordy. Overuses transition words (e.g., "additionally," "consequently"), making the text seem forced or redundant.
Overcapitalization	Overcapitalizes words in titles, bullets and initial references regardless of prompts to do otherwise.
Comma usage	Shows a preference for final serial commas and will insert them even against repeated instructions; seldom places a comma before "but" when needed.

Shortcoming	Description
Awkward sentence structures	Sometimes constructs sentences in an awkward or cumbersome manner (e.g., using "not only … but also" when "and" would suffice).
Voice shifts and inconsistent tone	Frequently shifts from the preferred active voice to passive constructions. Sometimes shifts tone inconsistently, leading to a disjointed reading experience.

You can attempt to address some of these limitations by refining your prompts, but don't expect a cure-all. As noted above, due to the way these AI tools are trained, their responses will tend to keep eplicating the same flawed results.

Conclusion

In concluding, we encourage you to embrace writing, making it a central part of your professional career.

Embrace the Evolution of Your Writing Journey

As we conclude our exploration of the art and science of effective business writing, it's important to remember that mastery in writing is not a destination but a continuous journey. This guide has equipped you with foundational techniques, advanced strategies, practical applications and insights into refining your craft. The true essence of writing excellence, however, lies in the perpetual practice, reflection and adaptation to new challenges and opportunities.

The call to action for you, as a reader and a practitioner of business writing, is to actively apply these principles in your daily communications. Experiment with different techniques, embrace feedback as a tool for growth and never shy away from revisiting the basics to reinforce your understanding. Writing is a craft honed over time through diligence, curiosity and an open mind.

Think of this guide as both a compass and a map, both providing direction and encouraging exploration. As language and business landscapes evolve, so too should your writing. Stay informed about emerging trends, adapt to the changing needs of your audience and continuously seek ways to enhance clarity, engagement and influence.

Above all, remember that everything you write is an opportunity to inform, persuade and inspire. Your journey in refining your writing craft shows commitment to excellence, professionalism and personal growth. So, embrace the challenges, celebrate the milestones and keep pushing the boundaries of what your writing can achieve. The world of business writing is vast and varied, and your unique voice can a powerful instrument within it. Keep writing, keep learning and let your words leave a lasting impression that transcends the confines of the page.

"No matter what anybody tells you, words and ideas can change the world."

— John Keating in *Dead Poets Society* (1989)

Appendices

Appendices

- Appendix 1: Grammar Fundamantals for Business Writing Excellence
- Appendix 2: Commonly Confused Words
- Appendix 3: Strategies for Ordering Data in Tables
- Appendix 4: Brief Introduction to Citations and References Using the APA Style Guide

Appendix 1: Grammar Fundamentals for Business Writing Excellence

This appendix provides a primer for those eager to gain a firmer grasp of foundational grammar terms and what they mean. It provides a concise overview of grammatical elements essential for crafting compelling business narratives, from the basic parts of speech to the intricacies of sentence structure. The primer will be especially helpful if you read other books on effective writing—most presuppose you are familiar with the following grammar terms.

Understand the basic parts of speech

The building blocks of any sentence—nouns, pronouns, verbs, adjectives and adverbs—are the foundation for expressing ideas clearly in writing.

Element	Type	Definition and example
Nouns	Common noun	Names general items. There are three types of common noun: concrete nouns, abstract nouns and collective nouns. (See examples under each subtype.)
	■ Concrete noun	A concrete noun names a tangible, physical thing. Example: "The **wind** scattered all the **pages** of the **report**."
	■ Abstract noun	Names ideas, qualities or states rather than concrete objects. Example: "Our **success** depends on **teamwork**."
	■ Collective noun	Names groups or collections of people or things. Example: "The **board** decides on the budget."
	Proper noun	Names particular people, places, entities or organizations. Example: "We analyzed **Google's** marketing strategy and reported it to our CEO, **Massimo Boss**, in **Paris**."

Element	Type	Definition and example
Pronouns	Personal pronoun	Pronouns replace nouns in sentences. Personal pronouns (I, you, he/she/it/they; me, you, him/her/it/them) make it possible to specify who or what the subject or object of a sentence is without using a common or proper noun.
		If I am talking to Sally, pronouns let me say "Did **you** know Desiree was a world-class runner? **She** won the Boston Marathon in 2018. Tony said **he** saw **her** medal. She has **it** in a display case." Without them, that sentence would have to read "Did Sally know Desiree was a world-class runner? Desiree won the women's division of the Boston Marathon in 2018. Tony said Tony saw Desiree's medal. Desiree has the medal in a display case."
Verbs	Action verb	Shows action. Example: "The team **developed** a new marketing plan."
	Linking verb	Connects the subject with a word that gives information about the subject. The verb "to be" is the most common, but others include "to feel," "to become" and "to seem" (among others). Example: "The results **seem** promising."
	Auxiliary verb	Helps the main verb express action or a state of being. Example: "We **have** completed the project." (The verb "have" is auxiliary, helping the verb "complete.")
	Modal verb	Expresses necessity or possibility. Example: "We **might** expand into new markets." (For more information, see "Use modal verbs (e.g., 'must,' 'should') to convey certainty and possibility" in Part 2).
Adjectives	N/A	Descriptive words that modify nouns. Example: "The **detailed** report offers valuable insights."
Adverbs	N/A	Modifiers for verbs, adjectives or other adverbs, often indicating how, when, where or to what extent. Example: "The team worked **extremely** efficiently."

Use sentence structure as the backbone of your writing

To create sentences, the building blocks described above must be used as subjects, predicates and objects.

Element	Type	Definition and example
Subject	N/A	The noun or pronoun performing the action or being described. Example: "The **manager** reviewed the report."
Predicate	N/A	The part of a sentence or clause containing a verb and stating something about the subject. Example: "The manager **approved the budget**."
Objects	Direct object	The noun or pronoun that receives the action of the verb. Example: "The manager reviewed **the proposal**."
	Indirect object	When a sentence involves actions of giving or telling, there can be a secondary, indirect object as well as a direct object. The direct object is what's given or told; the indirect object is the recipient. Example: "The manager sent **the team** an email."

Element	Type	Definition and example
Types of sentences	Simple sentence	Contains one and only one independent clause and no dependent clauses.[2] Example: "The meeting ended."
	Compound sentence	Contains two or more independent clauses, joined either by a comma and a conjunction or by a semicolon. Example: "The meeting ended, and the team felt relieved." (The comma and "and" separate two independent clauses.)
	Complex sentence	Contains an independent clause and one or more dependent clauses. Example: "The team felt relieved when the meeting ended." ("When the meeting ended" is a dependent clause: the independent clause "the meeting ended" has been rendered dependent by the presence of the subordinating conjunction "when" at its head.)
	Compound-complex sentence	Contains two or more independent clauses and one or more dependent clauses. Example: "The meeting ended, and the board voted to fund the project, which elicited cheers from the project team." ("The meeting ended" and "the board voted to fund the project" are independent clauses, and "which elicited cheers from the project team" is a dependent clause.)

Understand the distinction between restrictive (essential) and nonrestrictive (nonessential) clauses

Sometimes a descriptive clause says something about the thing it's describing that identifies the thing in a way that sets it apart from any other, similar things. In that case, it's called a restrictive (or essential) clause. Other times the clause just adds extra detail. In that case, it's called nonrestrictive (or nonessential). Which type of clause you're adding is signaled by presence or absence of commas, so be sure to use them appropriately.

Type of clause	Purpose	How it is formed	Example	Explanation
Restrictive (essential) clause	Provides essential, defining information	Follows directly after the thing it is modifying without a comma.	"Reports that contain errors need to be revised."	Only certain reports need to be revised: those that contain errors. The clause is essential to understanding which reports the speaker means.
Nonrestrictive (nonessential) clause	Provides extra information that is not essential	Is set apart from the rest of the sentence by commas.	"The CEO, whom I've known since our business school days, will be the keynote speaker."	The information about the CEO is extra detail; it is not intended to identify the CEO among other CEOs.

If the commas were removed from the example of the nonrestrictive clause, it would become a restrictive clause—in other words, the speaker would be identifying the CEO from among others by the fact that the two of them had been at business school together.

[2] Recall from Part 2 that (in a piece of grammatical circularity) an independent clause is defined as a subject and predicate that can stand alone as a sentence. A dependent clause is an independent clause that has lost its independence through the addition of a subordinating conjunction like "while" or "when" or a relative pronoun like "who," "which" or "that" at its head. It can no longer stand on its own.

Recognize verb forms used as nouns and modifiers, as well as appositives

Most people are familiar with nouns and verbs, but these less familiar parts of speech can be enlisted to help your writing shine.

Element	Definition	Example
Gerund	A verb ending in "-ing" when it is used as a noun.	"**Running** is a good form of exercise."
Present participle	A verb ending in "-ing" when it is used as a modifier.	"The **simmering** stew smelled delicious."
Past participle	A verb ending in "-ed," "-d," "-t," "en" or "n" and used as a modifier.	"The bridge was built with **reinforced** steel."
Infinitive	A verb's base form (the verb preceded by "to"), which can be used as a noun or a modifier.	"His goal is **to win**." (Infinitive used as a noun.) "He found a tomato **to pick**." (Infinitive used as a modifier, modifying "tomato.")
Appositive	A noun or noun phrase, set off by commas, that renames a noun directly preceding it.	"The CEO, **a visionary leader**, launched the new initiative."

Link ideas with conjunctions

Conjunctions link ideas and clarify relationships between different elements in your sentences, supporting smooth transitions and coherent arguments. Conjunctions can be categorized in the following way:

Type of conjunction	Definition	Example
Coordinating	Connects elements (words, phrases or independent clauses) that are equally important, logically and grammatically. Remembered by "FANBOYS": **for, and, nor, but, or, yet, so.**	■ "Apples **and** oranges" (Words.) ■ "The divorced men **but** not the unmarried women" (Phrases.) ■ "They were not prepared to admit they were surrounded, **so** they were unlikely to surrender." (Independent clauses.)
Correlative	Work in pairs to connect equal elements in a sentence. Common pairs are **both/and**, **either/or** and **neither/ nor**.	■ "**Both** the manager **and** the team were satisfied with the outcome."

Type of conjunction	Definition	Example
Subordinating	Links dependent clauses to independent clauses, introducing a condition or concession. Examples include **if, although, because, since** and **unless** (among others). If the dependent clause comes first, a comma separates it from the independent clause. If the independent clause comes first, no comma separates the two clauses.	**Before:** ■ "**Although** we finished the project, it was not implemented on time." ■ "**Because** she wanted to become a doctor, she took elective biology classes in high school." **After:** ■ "She took elective biology classes in high school **because** she wanted to become a doctor." ■ "You will not become an Olympic-level athlete **unless** you train regularly."

Show relationship between words with prepositions

Prepositions (words that usually precede a noun or pronoun and relate that word to another word or element in the clause) include such words as **about, across, among, before, below, between, during, from, in, into, off, near, to, until** and **with**. (There are many more.) The relationship they show can be understood as either a concrete or abstract spatial relationship.

■ **Example:** "The cup is **beside** the plate **on** the table."

"Beside" and "on" show the relationship of the cup, the plate and the table in physical space.

■ **Example:** "**Beneath** show of unity, there were signs of tension **between** the CEO and the board chair."

"Beneath" and "between" can indicate physical location, but here they show the abstract spatial relationship of the CEO and the board chair.

Appendix 2: Commonly Confused Words

With its expansive vocabulary, English is a powerful and flexible language, which makes it an excellent tool for communication. But its vast array of words with nuanced meanings can lead to pitfalls, especially when it comes to words that are easily confused due to their similar spellings, pronunciations or related meanings. Missteps in word choice can lead to misunderstandings that may undermine your credibility and obscure the message you intend to convey.

> "I'm your density. I mean, your destiny."
>
> — George McFly in *Back to the Future* (1985)

This appendix is a practical guide to navigating common linguistic challenges in the English language. It covers homophones, paronyms and other commonly confused words, as well as British and American English word variants. Each section provides examples of some of the most frequently confused words in the category, along with definitions and examples of correct use. (Note: The definitions focus on the meanings that are most likely to cause confusion or that are most commonly used. For those seeking more comprehensive definitions, consider consulting a dictionary, recognizing that, like style guides, dictionaries can differ in their interpretations.)

Hundreds more commonly confused words, defined and with examples of correct use, are also available as part of *Power in Precision*'s online content, which you can access online at www.powerinseries.com or by scanning the QR code.

Know the words that sound the same, but differ in meaning and spelling

Words that sound the same but differ significantly in meaning (though their spelling can be very close) are called homophones. For example, consider the pair **cent** and **scent**. **Cent** is a unit of currency, whereas **scent** is a smell or fragrance. They have the same sound, but a different spelling and meaning: they are homophones.

Below is a list of commonly confused homophones. Attentive readers will notice that some of the words have come up elsewhere in the book. They are included here so you will have access to all of the most commonly confused words in one place.

Words	Definition and example
Accept *or* **except**	**Accept** is receiving something willingly or to give admittance of approval to. Example: "We happily **accept** your proposal to buy our company."
	Except is the exception to a rule, pattern or opinion. Example: "Everyone's thrilled about the merger, **except** for Steve, who has concerns."
Affect *or* **effect**	**Affect**, as a verb, involves doing something that influences or causes a change to another thing or person. Example: "A new policy may **affect** employee morale."
	Effect, as a noun, refers to the outcome or result of an action. As a verb, it means to cause something to happen; to bring about. Example (noun): "The policy had a profound **effect** on the company's culture." Example (verb): "The new CEO aims to **effect** positive changes in company culture."
Capital *or* **capitol**	**Capital** means financial assets, or the city serving as the seat of government or administrative center. Example: "Our **capital** investment plans aim to boost growth."
	Capitol refers to a building or complex of buildings where a legislative body meets. Example: "Legislation affecting our country is debated in the **capitol**."
Complement *or* **compliment**	**Complement** is something that makes better or completes something else, or one of two mutually completing parts. Example: "This wine perfectly **complements** the flavors of the dish."
	Compliment is expressing praise or admiration. Example: "The CEO **complimented** the team for their innovative new product."
Discreet *or* **discrete**	**Discreet** involves maintaining privacy or subtlety, especially in sensitive situations, without causing embarrassment. Example: "Discussions about the potential acquisition were kept **discreet**."
	Discrete refers to distinct or separate elements and values. Example: "Our project was divided into three **discrete** phases for better management."
Hear *or* **here**	**Hear** refers to the act of perceiving or becoming aware of sound, gaining knowledge about something, or (in law) to give a listening to legal arguments. Example: "I **hear** your concerns about the new policy, and we will take them into consideration."
	Here means in or at this location, at this particular point, or present in life. Example: "Please sign the contract **here**, on the dotted line."
Hoard *or* **horde**	**Hoard** is to amass, often secretly, items or resources. Example: "The company decided to **hoard** supplies in anticipation of a market shortage."
	Horde refers to a large group, often used to describe a crowd or swarm of people or creatures, moving or acting collectively. Example: "A **horde** of investors crowded the conference hall to hear Warren Buffett speak."
Its *or* **it's**	**Its** indicates possession, belonging to "it." Example: "The company expanded **its** operations."
	It's is a contraction for "it is" or "it has." Example: "**It's** been a remarkable journey for the start-up."

Words	Definition and example
Liable, libel— *also confused in meaning with* **slander**	**Liable** refers to being legally responsible for something, especially in the context of wrongdoing or damages. Example: "Manufacturers are **liable** for harm caused by their products."
	Libel involves making a false and defamatory written or printed statement about someone. Example: "The magazine faced a **libel** lawsuit for the article published."
	Slander is making a false and defamatory spoken statement about someone. Example: "Accusations made during the argument amounted to **slander**."
Passed *or* **past**	**Passed** is past tense of "pass." Pass has many meanings, including to move, to go away from or beyond something, or to render or approve a decision. Example: "The new policy **passed** with overwhelming support."
	Past refers to a time that has already happened, or an event or occurrence that is behind someone in time. Example: "We've learned from our **past**."
Peace *or* **piece**	**Peace** refers to a state of tranquility, calmness or absence of conflict. Example: "The **peace** agreement was a major step forward in resolving the longstanding conflict."
	Piece refers to a part of a larger whole, or something of a specific class or kind. Example: "We need every **piece** of the puzzle to understand the complete market dynamics."
Peak, peek *or* **pique**	**Peak** signifies the highest point, or the maximum level of activity, capacity or value. Example: "Productivity hit its **peak** in the fourth quarter."
	Peek involves a quick or secretive look at something. Example: "He gave us a sneak **peek** of the new software."
	Pique refers to stimulating interest or curiosity. Example: "The announcement **piqued** everyone's interest in the new project."
Poor, pore *or* **pour**	**Poor** describes a lack of quality or an insufficient amount. Example: "The project's results were **poor** due to inadequate planning."
	Pore means to study or read something carefully. Example: "She **pored** over the documents to find the error."
	Pour involves transferring liquid from one container to another, to express thoughts freely or to supply freely. Example: "We **poured** our creativity into every campaign."
Principal *or* **principle**	**Principal** means the main or most important thing or person, a person in charge, or a primary or initial sum of money. Example: "The **principal** reason for the change was to cut costs."
	Principle is a fundamental belief or standard. Example: "Soren refused on principle to pay the unfair fine."

"In-famous is when you're MORE than famous. This man El Guapo is not just famous, he's IN-famous."

— Ned Nederlander in *¡Three Amigos!* (1986)

Words	Definition and example
Right, rite *or* write	**Right** means morally good, justified or correct. Example: "He made the **right** decision in approving the budget."
	Rite refers to a ceremonial or formal act, custom or practice. Example: "The company has a traditional **rite** for welcoming new employees."
	Write means to mark letters, words or other symbols on a surface, or to compose and send (a letter, message) to someone. Example: "Please **write** your feedback on the form provided."
Stationary *or* stationery	**Stationary** means not moving or not intended to be moved, fixed in one position or place. Example: "The **stationary** workstations in the factory enable the assembly line to operate smoothly and efficiently."
	Stationery refers to materials used for writing, such as paper, envelopes and pens. Example: "We need to order more **stationery** for the office, including paper for the printers."
Their, there *or* they're	**Their** indicates possession, showing that something belongs to them. Example: "**Their** new office is closer to downtown."
	There points to a location, matter or stage. Example: "Let's meet **there** at noon."
	They're is a contraction of "they are." Example: "**They're** expanding their operations next year."
To, too *or* two	**To** is a preposition used for expressing motion in the direction of (a place, person or thing). Example: "He is traveling **to** the conference next week."
	Too means also, or to an excessive degree. Example: "The project deadline is **too** tight for the current team."
	Two is the number following one and preceding three. Example: "We have **two** major clients in this region."
Who's *or* whose	**Who's** is a contraction for "who is" or "who has." Example: "**Who's** coming to the meeting?"
	Whose indicates possession, showing that something belongs to someone. Example: "**Whose** idea was this?"
Your *or* you're	**Your** signifies ownership or association, indicating that something belongs or relates to you. Example: "Is this **your** idea for the new campaign?"
	You're is a contraction for "you are." Example: "**You're** going to be the lead on this project."

Know words that look and sound similar, but differ in meaning and spelling

As seen above, homophones sound identical, but their meanings are very different. Paronyms, by contrast, are words that are close (but different) in pronunciation, spelling and also meaning. These words often share a common root, which can account for their similar—and yet distinct— meanings. For instance, consider **explicit** and **implicit**, which both derive from the Latin verb "explicare," meaning "to explain." The prefixes "ex" and "im" make all the difference here. "Ex" is a Latin preposition meaning "out of" or "from." Many words in English that start with "ex" (excavate, excise, excommunicate) have a sense of extraction, taking out. "Im," on the other hand, is a variant of "in," a prefix that comes from the Latin "in," meaning "in," "within," "into" or "toward." So **explicit** means something that is stated clearly—everything is out in the open, leaving no room for confusion. **Implicit**, by contrast, refers to something whose meaning remains within, without being directly stated.

The pair **historic** and **historical** is easier to understand because the common root (the word "history") is one we know. But the difference in the two words' meanings may be unfamiliar: **historic** means something significant in history, whereas **historical** simply relates to anything connected with history or past events.

Here are some examples of commonly confused paronyms:

Words	Definition and example
Adverse *or* **averse**	**Adverse** relates to acting against or contrary to something, or something being opposed to one's interests. Example: "Facing **adverse** market conditions last quarter, the company had weaker results than expected."
	Averse describes a personal dislike to something. Example: "I'm **averse** to taking unnecessary risks, especially with untested markets."
Advice *or* **advise**	**Advice** is a suggestion or recommendation regarding a decision or course of action. Example: "The best **advice** I got was to diversify investments."
	Advise is the act of giving a recommendation on what should be done. Example: "I **advise** we redirect our focus onto emerging technologies."
Allude *or* **elude**	**Allude** is to suggest or call attention to indirectly; to hint at. Example: "The CEO **alluded** to possible layoffs during the meeting."
	Elude means to escape the understanding or grasp of something, or to avoid or escape from someone or something, typically in a skillful or cunning way. Example: "The true cause of the issue continues to **elude** our team's analysis, requiring further investigation."
Allusion *or* **illusion**	**Allusion** refers to a subtle reference, often to something literary or cultural. Example: "The novel's title is an **allusion** to Shakespeare."
	Illusion involves a deceptive appearance or trick of the senses. Example: "The artist's **illusion** made the painting seem three-dimensional."
Assure, ensure *or* **insure**	**Assure** is about giving someone confidence, or to inform positively. Example: "I **assure** you, the project will be completed on time."
	Ensure means to make something certain or, occasionally, to guarantee an outcome. Example: "We have taken steps to **ensure** accuracy."
	Insure is to provide financial protection or make certain by taking necessary measures or precautions. Example: "It's wise to **insure** your car against accidents." Note: some style guides recommend limiting the use of insure to financial protection to avoid confusion with "ensure."
Breath *or* **breathe**	**Breath** refers to the air taken into or expelled when breathing. Example: "She took a deep **breath** before starting her presentation."
	Breathe means to take air into the lungs and then expel it. Example: "Remember to **breathe** slowly to stay calm during the meeting."

Words	Definition and example
Climactic *or* climatic	**Climactic** pertains to the peak or climax (most important moment) of something. Example: "The movie's **climactic** final scene shocked everyone."
	Climatic relates to climate, weather or atmospheric conditions. Example: "Our event planning takes **climatic** conditions into account."
Emigrate, immigrate *or* migrate	**Emigrate** means leaving one's country to live in another, focusing on the act of departure. Example: "Nino **emigrated** from Italy due to the war."
	Immigrate means entering a new country to live, emphasizing the arrival and integration into a new place. Example: "Kathryn and Mark **immigrated** to the United States for a new start."
	Migrate refers to the movement (temporary or permanent) from one place to another. Example: "The company decided to **migrate** its data to a cloud-based system to improve scalability and access for remote teams."
Eminent, immanent, imminent *or* preeminent	**Eminent** refers to a person who is distinguished and viewed as being above peers, through achievement or knowledge. Example: "The **eminent** scientist received a Nobel Prize."
	Immanent means remaining within or inherent, or present as a natural and permanent part of something. Example: "The company's commitment to innovation is **immanent** in its culture, influencing every aspect of its operations and decision-making processes."
	Imminent means to happen soon; in certain contexts, it can imply something bad or dangerous happening soon. Example: "The arrival of the storm is **imminent**."
	Preeminent refers to someone who surpasses others in their field or area; the highest in rank or importance. Example: "She is considered the **preeminent** expert in her field."
Farther *or* further	**Farther** generally relates to physical distance. Example: "How much **farther** is it to the next gas station?"
	Further applies to abstract or metaphorical advancement, such as deepening understanding or progressing in non-physical aspects. Example: "We need **further** discussion on this topic."
Penultimate *or* ultimate	**Penultimate** refers to the second-to-last item in a sequence. Example: "In our five-year plan, the **penultimate** year is crucial for laying the groundwork for our final expansion phase."
	Ultimate refers to the last or final item in a sequence, or something that is the best, greatest or most important. Example: "Our **ultimate** goal is to become the market leader in renewable energy solutions."
Precede *or* proceed	**Precede** means to come before something in time, order or position. Example: "An initial assessment will **precede** the project's full launch."
	Proceed means to continue or move forward with an action. Example: "The team will **proceed** with the implementation phase next week."

Know other commonly confused words

The English language is full of many other word pairs that are confused because people are unsure of which word is called for, grammatically, or because they're not sure which meaning goes with which word. A few are confusing because writers don't recognize that a two-word phrase that sounds identical to a single word actually means something different.

Below are some examples of word pairs that frequently cause confusion:

Words	Definition and example
Access or excess	**Access** refers to the means of approaching, entering or using something. Example: "The new software will allow employees to have easier **access** to important data."
	Excess means an amount that is more than necessary, permitted or desired. Example: "**Excess** inventory can be costly for the business."
All together or altogether	**All together** involves a group in unison. Example: "Let's sing the national anthem **all together**."
	Altogether refers to completely or in total. Example: "The project was **altogether** a huge success."
Among or amongst—also confused in meaning with between	**Among** refers to being amidst or in company of others, through the joint action of, or distributions involving entities or persons. Example: "Innovation is encouraged **among** all employees."
	Amongst is a more formal or British English variant of "among." Example: "There's a sense of camaraderie **amongst** the team members."
	Between means by common action, from one to another, shared by, or in relation to. Example: "The collaboration **between** the departments was successful." Note: Among, amongst and between can be used for two or more persons or entities. Between is especially appropriate to signify a one-to-one relationship, regardless of number involved.
Bring or take	**Bring** implies movement towards the speaker or reference point. Example: "Please **bring** your insights to our meeting."
	Take suggests movement away from the speaker or the initial location, or to remove something from its current location to another. Example: "You should **take** your laptop to the IT helpdesk."
Collaborate or corroborate	**Collaborate** means to work jointly with others, especially in an intellectual endeavor. Example: "The two companies decided to **collaborate** on the new project."
	Corroborate means to confirm or give support to a statement, theory or finding. Example: "The witness's testimony sought to **corroborate** the suspect's alibi."
Compose or comprise	**Compose** means to form by putting together. Example: "The advisory board is **composed** of representatives from finance, marketing and operations."
	Comprise means to be made up of. Example: "The advisory board **comprises** representatives from every department." Note: for advice on "comprised of," see the discussion on "compose" and "comprise" in Part 2's section on commonly confused words.

Words	Definition and example
Contiguous, continual *or* **continuous**	**Contiguous** refers to things that are next to, or in close proximity to, each other, sharing a common border or touching. Example: "The company acquired several **contiguous** properties to expand its distribution center."
	Continual means repeated or recurring actions or events with intervals or pauses between. Example: "Our **continual** improvement efforts help us adapt to the market."
	Continuous means unbroken or uninterrupted action or operation, without stops or breaks. Example: "Our support is **continuous** and unwavering."
Desert *or* **dessert**	**Desert** is a barren area of land where little precipitation occurs and living conditions are hostile. Example: "Few plants can thrive in the aridity of a **desert**."
	Dessert is a sweet course typically eaten at the end of a meal. Example: "Aurora had chocolate cake for **dessert**."
Elicit *or* **illicit**	**Elicit** is about drawing out a response or reaction, engaging in a way that encourages feedback or participation. Example: "Our customer survey aimed to **elicit** honest feedback on our services."
	Illicit refers to activities that are illegal or forbidden. Example: "The audit revealed **illicit** financial transactions that required immediate action."
Every day *or* **everyday**	**Every day** signifies something occurring daily, emphasizing repetition and regularity. Example: "Our team meets **every day** to discuss project progress."
	Everyday describes something commonplace or usual, fitting for routine or typical use. Example: "These reports are part of our **everyday** operations."
Fewer *or* **less**	**Fewer** is used to indicate a smaller number of persons or countable things. Example: "There are **fewer** apples in this basket than in the other."
	Less is used to indicate a smaller quantity or degree of uncountable things. Example: "She spent **less** time on this project than on the previous one."
Flaunt *or* **flout**	**Flaunt** is to proudly display achievements or possessions for all to see, unafraid to show off. Example: "She **flaunted** her success with a feature in the industry magazine."
	Flout is deliberately disregarding rules or conventions with a defiant stance. Example: "He **flouted** office dress code, opting for casual wear in formal meetings."
Good *or* **well**	**Good** describes something as adequate, suitable, pleasant or of good character. Example: "The feedback confirmed we made **a good** decision."
	Well is used primarily as an adverb to describe the manner in which actions are performed, indicating something is done to a satisfactory or commendable standard. It also often implies competence, thoroughness or health. Example: "Caden performs **well** under pressure, consistently delivering excellent results."
Imply *or* **infer**	**Imply** is when the speaker, writer or circumstance suggests something indirectly rather than stating it outright. Example: "By continually making reference to how scanty its funding was, Mark **implied** that the project might need more resources."
	Infer is when the listener or reader draws a conclusion from the information provided. Example: "From Mark's comments, I **infer** that the project needs more help."

Words	Definition and example
Irregardless *or* regardless	**Irregardless** is often mistakenly used for "regardless" but is considered incorrect in standard English.
	Regardless means despite everything, or not being affected by something. Example: "We will proceed with the plan **regardless** of the minor issues."
Laid, lay *or* lie	**Laid** is the past tense and past participle of lay, meaning something has been placed or put down. Example: "She **laid** the reports on the manager's desk yesterday."
	Lay is a verb that requires a direct object, meaning to place or put something down deliberately. Example: "Please **lay** the book on the table."
	Lie is a verb that does not require a direct object and is used to describe someone or something assuming a reclined position. "I like to **lie** down for an hour after work."
Lead *or* led	**Lead** is a present-tense form of a verb that means to guide or direct. Example: "He will **lead** the new initiative."
	Led, the past tense of "lead," describes having guided or directed in the past. Example: "She **led** a successful campaign last year."
Moot *or* mute	**Moot** points are debatable, or even irrelevant, to the current context. Example: "Arguing about budgets became **moot** after financial cutbacks."
	Mute refers to silence or the absence of sound, or an unwillingness or inability to speak. Example: "The conference call was on **mute** until everyone joined."
Quiet *or* quite	**Quiet** means making little or no noise, marked by little of no motion or (a person) not speaking. Example: "The office was unusually **quiet** after hours."
	Quite is used to indicate a degree of something. However, note that it can have nearly opposite meanings in American and British English. In American English, quite usually means "very" or "completely." Example: "The presentation was **quite** successful," meaning it was very successful. In British English, quite usually means "fairly" or "moderately," which is less intense. Example: "The presentation was **quite** successful," meaning it was moderately successful.
Than *or* then	**Than** is used in comparisons, helping to evaluate differences between people, places, things or ideas. Example: "Jill is a better hill climber **than** Jack."
	Then indicates a point in time, or the next in sequence of time. Example: "We'll finalize the design and **then** we'll proceed to the testing phase."
Wander *or* wonder	**Wander** is to move around without a specific direction or purpose, or to go astray. Example: "I like to **wander** through the local food markets."
	Wonder involves feeling amazement, curiosity or admiration. Example: "She couldn't help but **wonder** what the future would hold for her career."
Who *or* whom	**Who** refers to the person or people performing the action in the sentence. Example: "**Who** made this decision?" (Note: if you can replace who with "she" or "he," it is the correct choice.)
	Whom refers to the person or people receiving the action in the sentence. Example: "To **whom** should I address the letter?"

Be aware of other categories of words that you may encounter

If you decide to venture further into an exploration of words and their relationships, you are likely to encounter some of these categories into which words can be placed.

- **Antonym:** These are words that have opposite meanings. **Hot** and **cold** and **love** and **hate** are antonyms.

- **Contronyms (auto-antonyms):** These are words that have opposite meanings depending on the context in which they are used. This dual nature makes contronyms particularly fascinating. For example, the word **sanction** can mean both to approve or to punish, depending on the context. Another example is **dust**, which can mean to remove dust or to sprinkle something with dust.

- **Heterographs:** The words "heterograph" and "homophone" both point to words that are pronounced the same but have different meanings. Of these words, those that have different spellings are both heterographs and homophones; those that are spelled the same are homophones, but not heterographs. As it happens, all the words in the homophone section of this appendix are heterographs. Other heterographs include **flour** (a powdery substance used in baking) and **flower** (the blooming part of a plant) and **bear** (a large mammal) and **bare** (to uncover or expose). Examples of homophones that are not also heterographs are **bank** (a financial institution or side of a river) and **spring** (the season or a coil that bounces).

- **Homographs:** These are words that are spelled the same but have different meanings, and sometimes different pronunciations. **Lead** (to guide) and **lead** (a type of metal) are spelled the same but pronounced differently. Another example is **wind** (movement of air) and **wind** (to twist or turn).

- **Homonyms:** These are words that are both homophones (same pronunciation) and homographs (same spelling) but have different meanings. These words are a source of much of the richness and complexity in English, because they can lead to puns and wordplay. For example, the word **bat** can refer to a flying mammal or a piece of sports equipment. Similarly, **match** can mean a contest or to pair similar items.

- **Hypernyms and hyponyms:** Hypernyms are broader categories that encompass more specific words, known as hyponyms. For example, **sparrow** and **finch** are hyponyms in the hypernym **bird**, and **rose** and **lily** are hyponyms under the hypernym **flower**.

- **Polysemes:** These are words that have multiple related meanings. For example, **mouse** can refer to both a small rodent and a computer input device, with the latter taking its name from the former due to its shape and size. Similarly, **light** can refer to illumination, a lack of weight or a source of ignition.

- **Synonyms:** These are words that have the same or similar meanings. For example, **big** and **large** are synonyms that convey the same idea of size. Using synonyms is a great way to vary your language, avoid repetition and enhance the richness of your writing. Be careful, however, as many synonyms are different enough in connotation that they aren't interchangeable. "Grin," "smirk" and "leer" all come up as synonyms for "smile," but they have very different connotations.

Many words are members of more than one of these categories. **Bear**, for example, is a homonym (meaning an animal or to carry/support) and a heterograph (bear/bare).

Know the differences between American and British English

English is a global language, but it varies significantly depending on where it is spoken or written. British and American English, in particular, have developed noteworthy differences in spelling, vocabulary and even grammar. These variations can sometimes lead to confusion, especially for writers and readers who are accustomed to one form over the other.

Some word differences simply need to be known and remembered. For instance, while the British play professional **football** (what Americans call **soccer**) mainly on a Saturday, Americans will be playing their football (what the British call **American football**) mainly on a Sunday. Before the game, Americans might enjoy some **fries** (**chips** to the British—the crunchy snack known to Americans as **chips** are known to the British as **crisps**), grill some **eggplant** (the Brits' **aubergine**) or **zucchini** (**courgette**) and sip on a **soda** (**fizzy drink**). Dessert may include **candy** (**sweets**), **cookies** (**biscuits**), or, if a **vendor** (British: **seller**) is nearby, some **cotton candy** (**candy floss**). As they clean up afterward, Americans will discard items into the **garbage** or **trash**; the Brits will put them in the **rubbish**. As the author and editor of this book can both attest, it took them 20 years of marriage (to different partners) to master these differences, especially when eating out with friends from across the Atlantic.

Know spelling differences

Below are some common examples of spelling differences between American and British English. In each example, the American version is listed first:

- **Use of "ense" or "ence":** Words that in American English end in -ense often end in -ence in British English, as in **license/licence**, **offense/offence** and **defense/defence**.

- **Use of "er" or "re" at the ends of words:** American English often prefers "er," while British English uses "re." For example: **center/centre**, **fiber/fibre**, **liter/litre**, **meter/metre** and **theater/theatre**.

- **Use of one or two "l's":** This can be tricky, because the rules vary. In some cases, Americans use one "l" where the British use two: **canceled/cancelled**, **labeled/labelled** and **traveled/travelled**. In other cases, Americans use two "l's," where the Brits use one: **enroll/enrol**, **fulfill/fulfil** and **install/instal**. For correct spelling and formation of past tenses for your region, check an appropriate dictionary.

- **Use of "ize" or "ise" at the end of certain verbs:** American English often uses "ize" where British English prefers "ise" in verbs derived from Greek or Latin. For example, **analyze/analyse** and **characterize/characterise**. However, there are exceptions where the "z" spelling is also acceptable in British English, though less common. Examples include **organize**, **recognize** and **realize**. On the other hand, there are words where the switch to "z" is not typically accepted in British English, such as **criticise** (not **criticize**) and **paralyse** (not **paralyze**).

- **Fewer vowels in Amerian English:** American English tends to simplify spellings by dropping vowels, for example: **color/colour**, **honor/honour**, **labor/labour**, **maneuver/manoeuvre** and **gynecology/gynaecology**.

Some spelling differences don't follow a particular rule and just need to be remembered: **airplane/aeroplane**, **check/cheque**, **gray/grey**, **plow/plough**, **program/programme**, **toward/towards** and **yogurt/yoghurt**.

Know other grammatical differences

Throughout *Power in Precision*, we have touched on several other key differences between British and American English. Here's a summary of some important variations:

- **Collective nouns:** In American English, collective nouns (e.g., band, committee, company, family, government, staff, team) are often treated as singular, whereas in British English, they are usually plural.
  - **American English:** "The team **is** winning."
  - **British English:** "The team **are** winning."

- **Past simple/present perfect tense:** American English often uses the past simple tense where British English might use the present perfect.
  - American English: "I **already ate**."
  - British English: "I **have aleady eaten**."
  - American English: "**Did you see** the move yet."
  - British English: "**Have you seen** the movie yet."

- **Use of prepositions:** There are differences in preposition use, such as:
  - American English: "**On** the weekend."
  - British English: "**At** the weekend."
  - American English: "Different **from**."
  - British English: "Different **to**."
  - American English: "He lives **on** Main Street."
  - British English: "He lives **in** Main Street."

- **Punctuation:** The differences here are many, but the following are a few to keep top of mind:
  - **Period/full stop placement:** In American English, the period (or full stop) usually goes inside the quotation marks, while British English may place it outside, depending on the context.
    - American English: "Do you know the song? I think it's called 'Bad Romance.'"
    - British English: "Do you know the song? I think it's called 'Bad Romance'."
  - **Quotation marks:** American English typically uses double quotation marks for direct speech and quotations, while British English often uses single quotation marks. Then for quoted material within a quotation, each uses the other form of quotation marks:
    - American English: The teacher said, "The first three words of the US Constitution are 'We the People.'"
    - British English: The teacher said, 'The first three words of the US Constitution are "We the People".'

- **Use of subjunctive:** In simple terms, the subjunctive is used to express wishes, demands or suggestions that are not the current reality. American English retains the use of the subjunctive more frequently than British English
  - American English: "It is important that he **be informed**."
  - British English: "It is important that he **is informed**."
  - American English: "If I **were** you, I wouldn't do that."
  - British English: "If I **was** you, I wouldn't do that."

Appendix 3: Strategies for Ordering Data in Tables

This appendix goes into more depth on the strategies presented in the section "Structure data effectively in tables" in Part 3.

Ordinal ordering

For data that naturally falls into a sequence (e.g., ratings from excellent to poor), order columns or rows to reflect this sequence. This approach highlights trends and makes it easier for readers to follow the logical flow of data.

Example: Customer satisfaction survey results

Imagine you have data from a customer satisfaction survey in which customers rated various aspects of your service on a scale from "excellent" to "poor." Your table columns will reflect the labels on the scale, and the rows will reflect the survey items on which your service was rated. This ordering clearly shows the distribution of responses, making it easy to identify strengths and areas for improvement.

Service aspect	Excellent	Good	Average	Poor
Customer support	25%	50%	20%	5%
Product quality	30%	40%	25%	5%
Delivery speed	20%	30%	40%	10%

When the data doesn't have a natural order, several strategies can help you organize it effectively, as follows.

Alphabetical ordering

When there is no clear priority or sequence, alphabetical ordering (by row or column headers) can provide a neutral, easily navigable structure. When tables are listing individuals or organizations, the neutrality of alphabetical ordering sidesteps the problem of ego regarding listing location.

Example: Employee training programs

In a table listing employee training programs, where no other logical grouping applies, organize the programs alphabetically for ease of reference

Training program	Duration	Department
Communication skills	2 weeks	All
Data analysis	1 week	Marketing
Project management	3 weeks	Operations
Software proficiency	1 week	IT

Ordering by importance

If your audience will have a shared understanding of what's important, then ranking data according to its relevance or significance to the analysis makes sense. Data that is most critical to your argument or findings should be positioned to draw immediate attention.

Example: Marketing channel return on investment (ROI)

For a table analyzing the ROI for different marketing channels, order the channels from highest to lowest ROI to highlight the most effective strategies. This prioritization draws attention to the most profitable marketing channels. As in this example, ordering by importance tends to result an ordinal listing.

Marketing channel	ROI
Email marketing	200%
Social media	150%
TV advertising	120%
Traditional media	80%

Ordering conceptually

Arrange data based on conceptual categories or theories that relate to your topic (e.g., stages of the product lifecycle, as below). This method is useful when you want to highlight relationships or comparisons grounded in theoretical frameworks.

Example: Revenue from three products across product lifecycle stages

Product lifecycle stage	Product A	Product B	Product C
Introduction	$5,000	$7,000	$6,000
Growth	$20,000	$21,000	$35,000
Maturity	$30,000	$35,000	$60,000
Decline	$25,000	$28,000	$24,000

Ordering by observed data

Ordering data based on observed patterns or relationships within the dataset is particularly effective when the data reveals unexpected trends or clusters that you wish to draw attention to. The table below shows that while swimsuit sales at all locations peak in the summer months, the Lowell and Ann Arbor locations have a surge in February as well.

Example: Swimwear sales (in dollars) at four company locations, 2023

Location	Jan	Feb	Mar	Apr	May	Jun	Jul	Aug	Sep	Oct	Nov	Dec
Lowell MA	1950	3500	1950	2000	2000	3200	3100	2900	2000	2000	1950	1950
Ann Arbor MI	1900	3500	1900	1950	2000	3000	3000	2500	2000	2000	1950	1950
Salinas CA	2050	2200	2300	2500	2900	3500	3400	3000	2500	2500	2300	2400
Utica NY	2000	1900	1950	2000	2500	3300	3000	2500	2150	2100	2000	1900

Ordering by survey questions

For data derived from surveys or questionnaires, the survey or questionnaire itself may provide a suitable structuring mechanism for the table. Indeed, many surveys are designed in a logical manner, building on prior questions or sections, so mimicking that order in the tables can be highly beneficial.

Example: Employee satisfaction survey

Number	Question	Satisfied (%)	Neutral (%)	Dissatisfied (%)
1	Are you satisfied with your work environment?	70%	20%	10%
2	How do you rate work-life balance?	65%	25%	10%
3	Is the company culture positive?	80%	15%	5%

Mixed ordering for complex data

In tables presenting intricate datasets, a combination of strategies may be necessary. Start with the most critical organizing principle (e.g., order of importance) and then apply secondary criteria (e.g., alphabetical or empirical grouping) to structure the data effectively. For example, in a complex table showing sales performance by region, you might start with regions ordered by importance (total sales) and then alphabetically within each sales tier. This mixed approach highlights regions with the highest total sales while maintaining clarity within the table.

Example: Sales performance by region and highest-grossing nations per region

Region	Q1 sales	Q2 sales	Q3 sales	Total sales
North America	$50,000	$55,000	$60,000	$165,000
Canada	$16,000	$18,000	$18,000	$52,000
Mexico	$14,000	$15,000	$14,000	$43,000
United States	$20,000	$22,000	$28,000	$70,000
Europe	$40,000	$42,000	$45,000	$127,000
France	$12,000	$12,000	$13,000	$37,000
German	$15,000	$16,000	$17,000	$48,000
UK	$13,000	$14,000	$15,000	$42,000
Africa	$20,000	$25,000	$30,000	$75,000
Algeria	$3,000	$5,000	$7,000	$15,000
Egypt	$5,000	$7,000	$8,000	$20,000
South Africa	$12,000	$13,000	$15,000	$40,000
Asia	$20,000	$25,000	$30,000	$75,000
China	$12,000	$13,000	$15,000	$40,000
India	$5,000	$7,000	$8,000	$20,000
Japan	$3,000	$5,000	$7,000	$15,000

Appendix 4: Brief Introduction to Citations and References Using the APA Style Guide

Different disciplines use different style guidelines. In the business world and social sciences, the style guide of the American Psychological Association (APA) is widely used (*Publication Manual of the America Psychological Association*). Other style guides, including the Modern Language Association's *MLA Handbook*, the Associated Press's *Stylebook*, and the University of Chicago's *Chicago Manual of Style*, are also widely used. All of these are easily obtainable and offer online subscriptions.

You should adopt the one that suits your needs the best. Once you are familiar with one or several, you can also modify the guidelines they offer to suit your needs—just remember to be consistent and logical in your adaptations. Of course, if your organization has adopted a specific style guide or developed its own, you should refer to that to determine the correct way to cite and reference.

As discussed in "Support your main report with citations, references and appendices" in Part 4, there are two ways that writers cite sources in running text: through in-text citations or notes, either endnotes or footnotes. Note that even if in-text citations are being used for citing sources, the document may still have notes—it's just that the notes won't be used for citations.[3]

In-text citations can't be used without a reference list that provides full bibliographic information about the source. The reference list contains all the sources mentioned in in-text citations. Notes provide full bibliographic information, so there is no need for a reference list, but often a work that uses notes will also have a reference list or bibliography because it can be handy to have all the sources consulted listed in one place.

What follows is a very brief introduction to how in-text citations and entries in a reference list are styled using the APA style guide.

Adopt the correct approach to in-text citations

The exact way you cite sources in-text depends on the number of authors and the placement of the citation.

---

[3] If using footnotes or endnotes, put the note at the end of the sentence, directly after the sentence-final punctuation. Use ordinary Arabic numerals (1, 2, etc.), not Roman numerals (I, II, etc.). Although practice can be different in the sciences, use just one note per sentence. You can include multiple citations in one note.

Guidance on in-text citations

Citation type	Example
One author, citation is not part of the narration	"The organization had 20 years of data (Trounce, 2021)."
One author, citation is mentioned in running text	"In his study, Trounce (2021) found the organization had amassed 20 years of data."
Two authors, citation is not part of the narration	"More recent scholarship (Trounce & Fliss, 2023), however, shows little data."
Two authors, citation mentioned in running text	"In a more recent study, Trounce and Fliss (2023) noted a scarcity of data."

Note that when mentioning a work written by two authors in running text, the word "and" is written out, but in a parenthetical citation, an ampersand (an "&") is used.

For three or more authors, use "et al." This abbreviation means "and others." The period comes after "al"; there is no period after "et."

■ **Example:** "There is evidence (Kapoor et al., 2024) that the trend is reversing."

Sometimes an organization serves as an author.

■ **Example:** "The Federal Reserve is considering an interest rate cut (Federal Reserve, 2024)."

When multiple references are being cited parenthetically, they are separated by semicolons and listed alphabetically.

■ **Example:** "Many scholars and practitioners have weighed in on the phenomenon (Arvi, 2020; Bowen & Tish, 2018; Pew Charitable Trust, 2021; Winters et al., 2016)."

Adopt the correct approach to a reference list

The items in the reference list should correspond one-for-one with the items cited in your text. Don't leave any out, and don't include any sources not cited. Below are examples of certain common types of reference list entries.

Guidance on in-text citations

Source	Example	Details to note
Journal article	Smith, J., & Trujillo, M. (2021). Business trends: Impacts to note. *Journal of Business Essentials*, *12*(3), 45–67.	Only surnames are written out in full; all authors are given surname first. An article title is done in sentence capitalization (first word is capitalized, all other words are lowercased except for the first word after the colon and any proper nouns), with no quotation marks. Journal name is done in title capitalization (all words capitalized except conjunctions and prepositions) and italicized, as is the volume number. The issue number (in parentheses) is not italicized. Page numbers are given without "pp." or "pages."

Source	Example	Details to note
Magazine article	Doe, J. (2020, January). Maintaining anonymity in the modern world. *Modernity Today*.	Month and day (or just month, if no day) are given following the year. If the magazine has volume and issue number information, those are given as for a journal article.
Whole book	Silver, T. (2020). *Understanding the ins and outs of economics*. Economy Press.	The book title is in sentence capitalization and italics, and the name of the publishing company is given.
Chapter in a book	Nerf, B. B., Double, T., Whistle, G., & Indigo D. T. (2005). Having our say: A voice from the retail trenches. In V. Samrick & Wong, Q. (Eds.) *Voices from the workplace* (pp. 55–66), Sage Publications.	All the authors are listed, and a final serial comma separates the last author from the rest. All the editors are also named, with initials for the personal name and the surname written out in full, but with the surname last rather than first. For the book's editor or editors, the abbreviation "Eds." or (for one editor) "Ed." appears in parentheses before the book title. The book title and the chapter title are in sentence capitalization. The page numbers for the chapter are given in parentheses after the book title, prefaced by the abbreviation "pp." As with the other book example, the publishing company is included.

Those are only the most basic of reference types. Consult the APA manual for many more specific examples.

Exercises for Sharper Writing

Having explored the principles of effective business writing, this section turns to practice. The exercises reinforce clarity, structure and tone through focused editing and rewriting.

Exercises

- Exercise 1: Correct word choice, grammar and punctuation
- Exercise 2: Eliminate jargon and clichés
- Exercise 3: Rewrite for simplicity
- Exercise 4: Strenghten argument flow
- Exercise 5: Adapt tone to audience

Exercises for Sharper Writing

The following exercises invite you to apply the principles discussed in this book—clarity, precision, conciseness and audience awareness—to real examples. Each one focuses on a common challenge in business communication, such as grammar, word choice, tone and structure. Try editing the sentences or paragraphs yourself before reviewing the suggested revisions and explanations on the following pages. Treat these exercises as opportunities to practice writing that informs, persuades and inspires.

Exercise 1: Correct word choice, grammar and punctuation

Instructions: The following sentences contain common issues with word choice, along with common grammar and punctuation errors. Identify and correct the problems without rewriting the sentences for style and tone.

1. "Neither the new hires nor the manager are available for the meeting tomorrow."

2. During the meeting, Jane Smith, the Chief Financial Officer, discussed the company's growth strategy."

3. "With its staggering computational power, the tech team gave its instant approval to the new software."

4. "Recent changes in the market have had a positive affect on our revenue streams, enabling us to expand our operations faster than expected."

5. "We plan to launch the product next month the marketing team is preparing the materials."

6. "We are looking for a highly-motivated individual with strong problem solving skills to join our team."

7. "We are still waiting on feedback from the legal team, which we expect to receive by end of day."

8. "The Mikkelsen twin's company, Publishing.com, made them millionaires by age 25."

9. "Our goals are to improve customer engagement, expanded market share and increasing product quality."

10. "The deadline was extended, because we received additional requirements from the client."

Suggested revisions and explanations →

Suggested revisions and explanations

Mixed-up words

- **Original (#4):** "Recent changes in the market have had a positive **affect** on our revenue streams, enabling us to expand our operations faster than expected."

    - **Revision:** "Recent changes in the market have had a positive **effect** on our revenue streams, enabling us to expand our operations faster than expected."

    - **Explanation:** In its most common use, "affect" is a verb that means "influence or cause a change to a person or thing," whereas the most common use of "effect" is as a noun meaning "outcome or result of an action." In this sentence, we need the noun "effect" because the sentence describes the result of the market changes.

Subject-verb agreement

- **Original (#1):** "Neither the new hires nor the manager **are** available for the meeting tomorrow."

    - **Revision:** "Neither the new hires nor the manager **is** available for the meeting tomorrow."

    - **Explanation:** When "or" or "nor" are used, the verb following agrees in number with the noun directly preceding it. In this example, although "new hires" is plural, "manager" is singular, so "is" is the correct verb. If the order were reversed and "new hires" came directly before the verb, then "are" would be correct. ("Neither the manager nor the new hires are available for the meeting tomorrow.")

Run-on sentences

- **Original (#5):** "We plan to launch the product next month **the marketing team** is preparing the materials."

    - **Revision:** "We plan to launch the product next month**, and the marketing team** is preparing the materials."

    - **Alternative revision:** "We plan to launch the product next month**;** the marketing team is preparing the materials."

    - **Explanation:** Two independent clauses need to be separated by a comma and a conjunction (in this case, "and"). Alternatively, two independent clauses can be connected by a semicolon.

Incorrect apostrophe usage

- **Original (#8):** "The Mikkelsen twin**'s** company, Publishing.com, made them millionaires by age 25."

    - **Revision:** "The Mikkelsen twins**'** company, Publishing.com, made them millionaires by age 25."

    - **Explanation:** An apostrophe s after the word "twin" means that something belongs to just one twin. Here, the company belongs to both twins, so the apostrophe (and no additional s) should come after the word "twins."

Faulty parallel structure

- **Original (#9):** "Our goals are to **improve** customer engagement, **expanded** market share and **increasing** product quality."

- **Revision:** "Our goals are to **improve** customer engagement, **expand** market share and **increase** product quality."

- **Alternative revision:** "Our goals are **improved** customer engagement, **expanded** market share and **increased** product quality.

- **Alternative revision:** "Our goals are **improving** customer engagement, **expanding** market share and **increasing** product quality.

- **Explanation:** Parallel structure means all verbs should be in the same form. In each of the three corrections, "improve," "increase" and "enhance" all have the same verb form. It should be noted, however, that the meanings of the three corrections are slightly different. In terms of a statement of goals, the first is best because it is a statement of actions the company intends to take, whereas the other two are statements of conditions the company hopes to achieve.

Incorrect capitalization

- **Original (#2):** "During the meeting, Jane Smith, the **Chief Financial Officer**, discussed the company's growth strategy."

  - **Revision:** "During the meeting, Jane Smith, the **chief financial officer**, discussed the company's growth strategy."

  - **Explanation:** Titles should only be capitalized when they directly precede a person's name with the intention of being used as a form of address (e.g., "Chief Financial Officer Jane Smith"). When the title appears after the name, or in a general sense, it should be lowercased, as in the corrected example or as in the sentence "The company had the same chief financial officer for 15 years."

Hyphen usage

- **Original (#6):** "We are looking for a **highly-motivated** individual with strong **problem solving** skills to join our team."

  - **Revision:** "We are looking for a **highly motivated** individual with strong **problem-solving** skills to join our team."

  - **Explanation:** Compound adjectives like "problem-solving" need a hyphen when they appear before a noun. By contrast, adverbs like "highly" that end in "ly" should not be hyphenated.

Punctuation with "because"

- **Original (#10):** "The deadline was extended**,** **because** we received additional requirements from the client."

  - **Revision:** "The deadline was extended **because** we received additional requirements from the client."

  - **Explanation:** No comma is needed before "because" when it connects the cause to the action.

Preposition and article usage

- **Original (#7):** "We are still waiting **on** feedback from the legal team, which we expect to receive by **end of day**."

  - **Revision:** "We are still waiting **for** feedback from the legal team, which we expect to receive by the end of **the** day."

  - **Explanation:** "Waiting on" is informal; "waiting for" is more appropriate in a business context. Also, "end of day" needs the article "the."

Misplaced modifiers

- **Original (#3):** "With its staggering computational power, **the tech team** gave its instant approval to the new software."

  - **Revision:** "With its staggering computational power, **the new software** won the tech team's instant approval."

  - **Explanation:** "With its staggering computational power" refers to the new software, not the tech team, so "the new software" needs to follow comma after the modifying phrase.

Exercise 2: Eliminate jargon and clichés

Instructions: The following sentences are heavy with jargon and clichés that obscure their meaning. Rewrite each one using plain, specific language that communicates clearly and directly.

1. "In order to optimize our deliverables, we should touch base with key stakeholders to ensure alignment and maximize our value proposition moving forward."

2. "It's essential that we streamline our workflows to ensure we have best-in-class processes that will drive efficiencies and make it possible for us to scale effectively and achieve our growth objectives."

3. "We need to drill down into the data to identify low-hanging fruit that can be optimized for quick wins in the next quarter."

4. "Our goal is to ensure a seamless end-to-end process by utilizing cross-functional collaboration to break down silos and foster a more agile approach."

5. "It's important that we stay laser-focused on our KPIs, doubling down on what works and pivoting away from anything that doesn't move the needle."

"Our business is infested with idiots who try to impress by using pretentious jargon."

— David Ogilvy, advertising executive and founder of Ogilvy and Mather

---

Suggested revisions and explanations →

Suggested revisions and explanations

1. **Original:** "In order to optimize our deliverables, we should touch base with key stakeholders to ensure alignment and maximize our value proposition moving forward."

    ■ **Revision:** "We should meet with key stakeholders to bring everyone into agreement so we can improve our results."

    ■ **Explanation:** We substitute the simpler phrase "improve our results" for jargon ("optimizing deliverables," "maximize our value proposition") that are both talking about improving what the organization offers its customers or clients, and we replace "touch base" with the more straightforward "meet."

2. **Original:** "It's essential that we streamline our workflows to ensure we have best-in-class processes that will drive efficiencies and make it possible for us to scale effectively and achieve our growth objectives."

    ■ **Revision:** "We need to simplify our workflows and improve our processes so we can grow and meet our goals."

    ■ **Explanation:** We remove clichés ("best-in-class," "drive efficiencies") and focus the message on the need for simplification and process improvement.

3. **Original:** "We need to drill down into the data to identify low-hanging fruit that can be optimized for quick wins in the next quarter."

    ■ **Revision:** "We need to analyze the data to find easy improvements we can make for quick results next quarter."

    ■ **Explanation:** We replace corporate jargon ("drill down into data," "low-hanging fruit") with straightforward language about using data to find easy improvements for quick results.

4. **Original:** "Our goal is to ensure a seamless end-to-end process by utilizing cross-functional collaboration to break down silos and foster a more agile approach."

    ■ **Revision:** "We aim to create a smooth process by working together across teams and adopting a flexible approach."

    ■ **Explanation:** We replace corporate buzzwords ("seamless," "end-to-end") with a single adjective ("smooth") and replace overly abstract ("cross-functional collaboration") and distractingly metaphoric ("breaking down silos") jargon with a clear statement of what that jargon means ("working together across teams") to better highlight the goal of creating smooth processes through teamwork and flexibility.

5. **Original:** "It's important that we stay laser-focused on our KPIs, doubling down on what works and pivoting away from anything that doesn't move the needle."

    ■ **Revision:** "We need to focus on our key metrics, doing more of what works and less of what doesn't."

    ■ **Explanation:** We replace clichés ("laser-focused") and business jargon ("pivoting away") with clearer language, encouraging a focus on key metrics and successful projects.

Exercise 3: Rewrite for simplicity

Instructions: The following sentences are needlessly formal or complex. Rewrite each one in plain English so the meaning is clear and direct.

1. "Following the conclusion of the project, a post-implementation review will be conducted to identify potential areas for continuous improvement."

2. "The newly introduced compliance regulations necessitate a reevaluation of our existing protocols to ensure our adherence."

3. "We must leverage market segmentation data to tailor our content to ensure that our messaging resonates with the target demographics.""

4. "The process of integrating the two systems, which will involve the alignment of various technical components, will ensure seamless interoperability and functionality."

5. "Our objective is to mitigate potential risks by instituting a robust governance framework that addresses the evolving regulatory landscape."

"The finest language is mostly made up of simple, unimposing words."

— Mary Ann Evans, writing under her pen name, George Eliot

Suggested revisions and explanations →

Suggested revisions and explanations

1. **Original:** "Following the conclusion of the project, a post-implementation review will be conducted to identify potential areas for continuous improvement."

    - **Revision:** "After the project, we'll review it to find ways to improve."

    - **Explanation:** The original wording was formal, wordy and unnecessarily passive ("a post-implementation review will be conducted" can be stated simply as "we'll review"; "post-implementation" is already covered by "after the project"). The revised sentence is shorter and more direct. It implies efficiency and commitment.

2. **Original:** "The newly introduced compliance regulations necessitate a reevaluation of our existing protocols to ensure our adherence."

    - **Revision:** "The new rules mean we need to review our processes to confirm they comply."

    - **Explanation:** The original was complex and wordy; the revised sentence uses simpler, more direct language and cuts out unnecessary words.

3. **Original:** "We must leverage market segmentation data to tailor our content to ensure that our messaging resonates with the target demographics."

    - **Revision:** "We must use data on different market segments to adjust our content so it appeals to our various customers."

    - **Explanation:** Unnecessary jargon is replaced by a simpler way of saying that the company needs data on different customer groups so it can make its content appealing to them.

4. **Original:** "The process of integrating the two systems, which will involve the alignment of various technical components, will ensure seamless interoperability and functionality."

    - **Revision:** "Integrating the two systems, a highly technical process, will result in the systems working together smoothly."

    - **Explanation:** The technical detail about alignment is summarized, and jargon ("seamless interoperability and functionality") is replaced by a simple, overarching statement of the result ("systems working together smoothly").

5. **Original:** "Our objective is to mitigate potential risks by instituting a robust governance framework that addresses the evolving regulatory landscape."

    - **Revision:** "We aim to reduce risks by setting up strong governance that adapts to changing regulations."

    - **Explanation:** The original sentence is shortened and simplified.

Exercise 4: Strengthen argument flow

Instructions: The arguments in the following paragraphs are hard to follow. Restructure them so the reasoning is clear and flows naturally to a logical conclusion.

1. Our team has worked really hard to improve the user interface of the app, which is something we've heard about a lot from users. The market for apps like ours is growing fast, and it's crucial we stay competitive. We need to focus on making the app easy to use, and this will help us get more users. Also, we should think about new features to add.

2. The project failed because we didn't hit our targets, and the team didn't communicate well. Although we had some good ideas, our execution wasn't great. The timeline was too short, and we didn't allocate enough resources. However, we should keep these ideas for the next project, but it's important to avoid the same mistakes.

3. We should expand our presence in emerging markets because they offer huge potential for growth. The company's resources are limited, and competition is fierce in these regions. We can't ignore the opportunity, and our competitors are already taking action. It will be challenging, but the potential rewards are significant.

4. Our customer service scores have been dropping, but we've also been cutting costs. We know that quality service is important to retain customers. Employees are feeling overworked, and some customers have complained about long response times. Increasing our investment in training would help, but it could be expensive.

5. Our latest advertising campaign reached a lot of people, but the sales numbers didn't increase as expected. The message was clear, and we used multiple channels, but we might not have targeted the right audience. Sales should have improved. The timing of the campaign could have been better, too.

"The shorter and the plainer the better."

— Beatrix Potter, author, natural scientist and conservationist

---

Suggested revisions and explanations →

Suggested revisions and explanations

1. **Original:** "Our new product is innovative, and customers are always looking for something fresh. The market is becoming more competitive, and we need to maintain our position. Therefore, it's important to invest in marketing to make sure our customers know about it. The features are unique, and we believe it will attract a lot of attention."

    ■ **Problems with original:** The paragraph has two potential topic sentences (the first and second sentences), but a good paragraph should develop only one. Furthermore, the ideas jump around without a clear connection between product innovation, customer needs, competition and the need for marketing.

    ■ **Revision:** "Our new product offers unique features that will stand out in a highly competitive market, and our fresh approach is sure to drive sales—provided the public is made aware of our offering. Marketing is essential to accomplish this and to maintain and expand our position. "

    ■ **Explanation:** The new paragraph combines the concepts from the first and fourth sentence for a new topic sentence. Marketing is highlighted in the second sentence as necessary for even an innovative product to succeed.

2. **Original:** "The project failed because we didn't hit our targets, and the team didn't communicate well. Although we had some good ideas, our execution wasn't great. The timeline was too short, and we didn't allocate enough resources. However, we should keep these ideas for the next project, but it's important to avoid the same mistakes."

    ■ **Problems with original:** The causes of the project's failure are given in an incoherent manner, apparently without recognition of how some of the causes (short timeline) lead to others (missed targets). The recommendation to keep the ideas behind the project is made without any justification, and the counsel to avoid repeating the same mistakes rings hollow without recommendations on how to do that.

    ■ **Revision:** "Despite strong ideas behind it, the project failed due to insufficient planning, a rushed timeline that resulted in missed targets, poor team communication and inadequate resource allocation. Moving forward, we should retain the ideas but set realistic deadlines, fund the project adequately and improve communication to avoid repeating the same mistakes."

    ■ **Explanation:** The paragraph now leads with the statement that the ideas behind the project are good, which justifies the recommendation to retain them. Cause and effect are established between two aspects of the failure (a rushed timeline and missed targets). The suggested solution addresses each of the causes of failure rather than merely saying that the causes should be avoided.

3. **Original:** "We should expand our presence in emerging markets because they offer huge potential for growth. The company's resources are limited, and competition is fierce in these regions. We can't ignore the opportunity, and our competitors are already taking action. It will be challenging, but the potential rewards are significant."

    ■ **Problems with original:** The paragraph mixes opportunities and challenges without establishing a clear position or a prioritized argument about why expansion is necessary.

    ■ **Revision:** "Emerging markets present a significant growth opportunity that we cannot afford to overlook. While our resources are limited and competition in these regions is fierce, the long-term rewards outweigh the risks. If we do not want to cede these high-potential markets to our competitors, we must take strategic action to secure our position."

    ■ **Explanation:** The revised paragraph states the opportunity offered by emerging markets, then acknowledges the challenges while asserting that the benefits outweigh the risks. It concludes with a warning of what will be lost if the company does not seize the opportunity.

4. **Original:** "Our customer service scores have been dropping, but we've also been cutting costs. We know that quality service is important to retain customers. Employees are feeling overworked, and some customers have complained about long response times. Increasing our investment in training would help, but it could be expensive."

   - **Problems with original:** The paragraph discusses various factors that contribute to declining customer service, but it lacks a clear flow and resolution on how to address the problem effectively.

   - **Revision:** "Our declining customer service scores are the result of cost-cutting measures, which have led to overworked employees and slower response times. To improve, we need to invest in employee training, which will enhance service quality and help retain customers. While this will require additional resources, the long-term benefits of improved customer satisfaction and loyalty will outweigh the costs."

   - **Explanation:** The alternative states directly that cost-cutting measures are responsible for declining service and provides a clear solution (training), explaining the rationale for investing resources despite potential costs. It offers a clear progression from problem to solution.

5. **Original:** "Our latest advertising campaign reached a lot of people, but the sales numbers didn't increase as expected. The message was clear, and we used multiple channels, but we might not have targeted the right audience. Sales should have improved. The timing of the campaign could have been better, too."

   - **Problems with original:** The paragraph lists reasons for the campaign's mixed results but lacks a cohesive explanation or conclusion about why sales didn't improve.

   - **Revision:** "Although our advertising campaign reached a broad audience and delivered a clear message, sales did not increase as anticipated. The issue likely lies in targeting: we may not have reached the right audience for this product. Additionally, the timing of the campaign may not have aligned with market demand. Going forward, we should refine our targeting strategy and schedule campaigns more strategically to achieve better results."

   - **Explanation:** The alternative clarifies why sales didn't improve and concludes strongly by offering ways (refining targeting, adjusting timing) to address the issues.

Exercise 5: Adapt tone to audience

Instructions: Each scenario below lets you practice adapting tone, formality and the level of detail for different audiences. Write a short paragraph (roughly 50–70 words) on the given topic for each recipient type—executive, peer and client. A sample response follows the scenarios.

- **Scenario 1: Policy update:** You need to inform stakeholders about a significant update to a policy.
  - **Executive:** Explain how the updated policy aligns with the organization's strategic goals, legal obligations or industry standards, and highlight the intended effect on organizational performance or compliance.
  - **Peer:** Detail the practical implications of the policy change, such adjustments on workflows, and outline how you need their support in implementation.
  - **Client:** Reassure them that the updated policy is designed to enhance service quality or improve outcomes, while addressing any potential concerns about the transition.

- **Scenario 2: Budget request:** You need to request additional budget for an ongoing project.
  - **Executive:** Focus on the return on investment and how the additional budget will contribute to achieving strategic business goals.
  - **Peer:** Detail the specific areas where the budget is short, explaining why additional funds are necessary to complete project tasks.
  - **Client:** Explain how the budget will enhance the project's value to them without focusing too much on internal financials.

- **Scenario 3: Change in leadership:** You need to announce that a key leader in the organization is leaving and being replaced.
  - **Executive:** Frame it in terms of business continuity, strategic vision and any adjustments to organizational priorities.
  - **Peer:** Emphasize day-to-day consequences such as how workflows might change and who the interim contact will be.
  - **Client:** Reassure them of continued service quality and a smooth transition, introducing the new leader with relevant credentials.

"The most important thing to remember is you must know your audience."

— Lewis Howes, author and podcaster

Sample answer →

Sample answer

Project deadline extension: You need to inform the audience that a project deadline will be extended due to unforeseen challenges.

Executive

In communicating with an executive, it's essential to maintain a high-level, strategic tone. The message should focus on the overall business impact of the delay, while conveying control and alignment with long-term goals:

- **Example:** "We've encountered unexpected technical challenges with the new software implementation that will require extending the project timeline by two weeks. While this adjustment will delay the initial rollout, it allows us to address the underlying issues so we have effective integration across the platform. We're confident this extension will better position us to achieve the long-term objectives of an enhanced user experience and reduced operational downtime, contributing to our overall growth strategy."

Peer

For a peer, a more collaborative tone is appropriate. You will give the peer more details on the operational or technical reasons for the delay than you gave to the executive. Highlighting joint efforts and next steps will keep the tone collegial and solution-oriented:

- **Example:** "The integration module is taking longer than expected to finish due to some unforeseen compatibility issues with our existing system. We've been troubleshooting with the vendor, but the additional work will push the deadline back by two weeks. We're focusing on the remaining tasks and reassigning resources to minimize disruption. Let's coordinate on how this impacts the rest of the workflow and adjust our activities accordingly."

Client

When addressing a client, it's crucial to strike a reassuring tone, focusing on maintaining trust and prioritizing their needs. Emphasize the quality of the outcome and the commitment to delivering a solution that meets their expectations:

- **Example:** "We wanted to inform you that due to some unforeseen technical issues, we need to extend the project deadline by two weeks. The extra time will allow us to make sure the final deliverable meets the high standards we've set for your project. We're fully committed to delivering a solution that's both reliable and effective. We'll keep you updated on progress throughout this final phase. Rest assured, your needs remain the focus of our efforts."

* * * * *

Bringing it together

Sharper writing comes from habit as much as knowledge. If you revisit these exercises periodically—reworking examples, rewriting emails or reviewing real workplace documents—you'll find that clarity and conciseness become second nature. Every sentence you revise is a step toward writing that earns attention and conveys authority.

Index

Power in Precision strives to make writing advice accessible by minimizing the use of grammatical formalities and terms where possible. This approach is reflected in our index. Although some entries do involve grammatical terms, the majority are crafted in the same clear, accessible language as the book itself. We have tailored the index to focus on ease of use and comprehension, balancing traditional indexing standards with our goal of clarity.

O

P

Q

U

V

W

Y

About the Author

With over three decades of experience, Mark Watson excels in financial services, governance and risk management. His career spans influential roles working with Britain's Conservative Party, the Adam Smith Institute, McKinsey & Company, Moody's, Tapestry Networks and EY.

Mark has been writing throughout his career, whether responding to proposed legislation, producing leading industry surveys or creating action-oriented reports for investors, board directors and senior executives. He has covered a wide array of topics, including governance, risk management, digital transformation and many more.

Mark has written and edited millions of words, created thousands of data-rich charts, presented at hundreds of events and written and ghostwritten speeches. He has navigated through thousands of redlined edits of his writing. He has drawn on these experiences in writing *Power in Precision*.

He lives in Concord, Massachusetts—a fitting home for a UK/US dual national, given its historical significance as the birthplace of the American Revolution.

Acknowledgements

Writing is important to me. Back in high school, I disliked English intensely. I found writing laborious and couldn't see why it mattered. It was only at college, during my third year working in politics, that I realized being a good writer sets you apart. Being smart is helpful, but not if you can't communicate those ideas, especially in written form. So, over time, I taught myself to write effectively and instinctively.

I have had the fortune of working with some great writers and editors. At the Adam Smith Institute, Eamonn Butler and Madsen Pirie would drop off hand-edited manuscripts for me to input, and I'd labor over why they made the editing choices they did. I ran the gauntlet of the *McKinsey Quarterly* editorial team several times and learned you have to make every word count. Colleagues at Moody's drove home the importance of active voice and making words inform action. Debra Greenberg drilled into me the importance of precision and consistency. Francesca Forrest, the editor of this book, educated me on writing through her many edits and comments explaining those edits. *Power in Precision* is better because of Francesca's dedication to making it accessible and authoritative.

I read a lot, too. At college, I had *The Economist*, *Newsweek* and *Time* delivered. The main reason was to stay current, but the effect was that I was immersed in excellent writing. The countless business books I read provided further enrichment. I owe many journalists, writers and editors for this free writing education.

I'm still learning. On numerous occasions while writing *Power in Precision*, I came to realize why certain grammar changes are made or why grammarians wage decades-long debates on seemingly trivial matters (some are, some aren't). Compiling the appendix on commonly mixed-up words revealed several mistakes I have made routinely over three decades. I'm grateful for this lifelong learning experience.

Most of all, I'm profoundly grateful for my family: for Kathryn, my wife, and our wonderful children, Soren, Aurora and Caden. They make life worth it. Kathryn deserves special thanks. She has let me wind my way through my atypical career, knowing that I can't thrive without change and new challenges. She understands how important writing is to me and has indulged me, allowing me time and space to write *Power in Precision* and its sister *Power In* books on data visualization, presentations and business conversations, still in the works. Without Kathryn's patience and love, I'd have stalled in my twenties.

www.ingramcontent.com/pod-product-compliance
Lightning Source LLC
Chambersburg PA
CBHW080750120626
46557CB00005B/1219